## Notes & Apologies:

★ Subscriptions to *The Believer* include four issues, one of which might be themed and may come with a bonus item, such as a giant poster, art object, or free radio series. View our subscription deals at *thebeliever.net/subscribe*.

★ Congratulations to *Believer* contributor and McSweeney's author Ahmed Naji, as well as translator Katharine Halls, whose book *Rotten Evidence: Reading and Writing in an Egyptian Prison* is a finalist for the National Book Critics Circle Award in Autobiography. Make haste to your local independent bookstore to pick up a copy. Also, look out for a future story from Ahmed in these pages, wherein he visits Michael Heizer's massive land-art project in Garden Valley, Nevada.

★ This issue's cover depicts, clockwise from the top left, Jenny Slate, Marcus Thompson II, Monica Padman, and Sissy, one of Greer Lankton's most beloved dolls.

★ We would like to express our gratitude to whoever sent us a babka directly to the office. We don't know who did this but we are very appreciative. And it should be noted that we would welcome any future babkas, as well. Thank you.

★ The spot illustrations here and there in this issue, of daily moments observed in New York City, are by Matt Panuska.

# DEAR THE BELIEVER

849 VALENCIA STREET, SAN FRANCISCO, CA 94110

*letters@thebeliever.net*

**Dear Believer,**

When my son went away to college, he told me he planned to major in biomedical engineering but focus on pursuing his lifelong passion for opera. How he fell in love with opera is a whole other story, which I won't get into, but which involves a man we befriended on the California Delta one summer who lived on his boat, smoked a pipe, and basically ate only fruit. We used to spend every summer on the Delta, and we met a lot of interesting people there. In any case, as a young musician, my son became enamored with opera. But it was so removed from the zeitgeist, he felt that only a complete reimagining could bring it to the forefront of cultural discussions, and thus his senior thesis was an "avant-garde" opera that he hoped would prove the relevance of an evolving art form. As he slogs through grad school (in engineering, not opera), I was so pleased to see his undergraduate zeal validated and celebrated in the music issue (Winter 2023). I hope Rhiannon Giddens's work is the beginning of renewed excitement about the genre.

*Milton Jones*
*Inverness, CA*

**Dear Believer,**

Niela Orr's "Resurrector" column on *Glitter* (Winter 2023) was a pleasure. I think it's a testament to Mariah Carey's artistic talent that she could distill the film's glitzy, neon-infused aesthetic and clichéd plot into a hard-hitting soundtrack that remains full of bops in 2024. It's as if Carey sifted through a dumpster, scavenged the redeemable scraps, and then pieced them together into a beautiful assembly of dilapidated parts. They do say that constraint can be one of the most valuable creative tools. Sometimes it's good to have limits, and to have to figure out how to work around them and with them. I've certainly found this in my own creative work.

*Jasper Cerone*
*New York, NY*

**Dear Believer,**

Because I am an elementary school music teacher, my ears are well trained to tolerate most any noise. There is, however, one instrument I will never allow in my classroom, and it is the kazoo ("A Brief and Annoying History of Kazoo Orchestras," Winter 2023). It is an infernal creation. I can only give thanks that kazoo bands went out of style long ago—and thank goodness the US government put the kibosh on any claims to musicality put forth by kazooers! "A kazoo is not a musical instrument"—I've been saying this for *years*! Glad I have the weight of the feds behind me on this one.

*Kim Wilson*
*Vergennes, VT*

**Dear Believer,**

In Will Epstein's interview with Nathaniel Dorsky (Fall 2023), the filmmaker mentions a San Francisco dentist who administers nitrous oxide to patients as they recline in dental chairs "located in a greenhouse in the backyard with tropical plants and music." I, too, want to feel like I'm "sitting on one of the rings of Saturn" while getting my teeth cleaned. It sounds like a spiritual experience, not unlike watching Dorsky's films. Please reveal to us, your dear readers, the name of this dentist.*

*Michelle R*
*Oakland, CA*

**Dear Believer,**

Glad to see Pap smears shouted out in last issue's crossword (Winter 2023). Take care of your reproductive health, people!

*Oona Moore*
*Missoula, MT*

**Dear Believer,**

I have never been moved to listen to BTS. Not even a little. Not until I read Mimi Lok's Jungian exploration of the band's work ("In Search of Wholeness with BTS," Winter 2023). I'm a sucker for anything that can drive self-exploration on this deeper, messier level. So thank you to Lok for helping people like me discover something new.

*Natalia Benedetto*
*San Francisco, CA*

---

* Editors' Note: We can't reveal the name in print, because… well, you can guess why. But if you look hard enough, you'll find him.

**BLVR:** In *In the Distance* you
describe the desert beautifully. Did
you spend much time there as a
visitor?

**HD:** I'm almost Oulipian in
private, quirky, personal ways
that are meaningless to people
other than me. I set weird rules
for myself. Sometimes I don't
realize they are in place until I'm
confronted with them over and
over again. With *In the Distance*,
one very overt rule was that I'm
not going to go and have an air-
conditioned experience of those
spaces from, like, a Ford Focus or
whatever. [*Laughter*]

**BLVR:** There's a geographic
idiosyncrasy to this painting that's
eloquent for me as a Canadian...
Can you talk a bit about Canada as a
milieu in your work?

**KM:** This to me is North
America. The border is recent;
it's pretty arbitrary. And so many
Indigenous people would have
moved around and across it. For
foliage, often I'm looking at how
other painters paint plants. For
instance, these were all based
on John James Audubon, an
early-nineteenth-century North
American botanical painter who
painted a lot of birds and their
environments. I wanted to have
Western science and Indigenous
cosmology collide in order to
discuss the science that's embedded
in our ways of knowing about all
parts of nature, whether it's star
knowledge or plant knowledge.

*Compiled by Lia Sina; illustrations by Kristian Hammerstad*

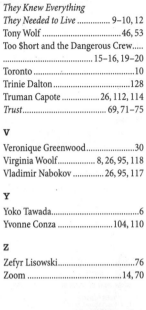

"THAT'S NOT THE SHOW. THE SHOW ISN'T THE VIEW." *p. 95*

"BUT MORE THAN THAT, GREER WAS A DOLL HERSELF: A DOLL WHO MADE DOLLS, A DOLL SURROUNDED BY DOLLS, ALIVE OR NOT." *p. 86*

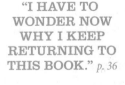

"I HAVE TO WONDER NOW WHY I KEEP RETURNING TO THIS BOOK." *p. 36*

*Photo by Greer Lankton, 1980s. Courtesy of The Greer Lankton Collection, Mattress Factory Museum, Pittsburgh, PA.*

# UNDERWAY

## WE ASK WRITERS AND ARTISTS: WHAT'S ON YOUR DESK? WHAT ARE YOU WORKING ON?

*by Jordan Kisner*

**Photograph**

*Years ago I ran a production company called The Bellwether, which worked with young artists to show their work in multidisciplinary ways. My first collaboration was with a friend, the dancer and photographer Devin Alberda. This is a photo we used in that show, which Devin took at the New York City Ballet.*

**Stack of books**

*I love diaries, and I've been studying the diaries of the visual artist Anne Truitt. I found this collection for five dollars at the Montague Bookmill, in Massachusetts, which might be my favorite bookstore. It definitely has my favorite slogan: "Books you don't need in a place you can't find."*

**Tiny vase with pens**

*Circa 2019, I got tired of looking at a screen all the time and took a pottery class to play around with something tactile. As it happens, nothing I made turned out except this tiny lopsided vase, which now holds pencils.*

**Plain white sticky notes and notecards**

*I keep these with me everywhere—the sticky notes for lists or stray thoughts, and the notecards for recording ideas or sketches for writing projects.*

**Map**

*This is a copy of an old topographical map of the Rondout Reservoir in the Hudson Valley. The black dots show buildings and homes that were sunk underwater to supply New York City with drinking water. I got this while researching a story but have kept it because I like the look of the wavy lines and the idea of mapping what's already sunk.*

**Yoko Tawada's The Emissary**

*One of my best friends sent me this for my birthday. I had given her Claire Keegan's novella Foster for hers, with a note saying it had provided my favorite one-gulp reading experience of 2023, so she replied with the novella that had done the same for her.*

**Postcard in a frame**

*I had the honor of interviewing a personal hero, the poet Mary Ruefle, for my podcast, Thresholds. Mary doesn't have a computer or email, so I wrote a paper thank-you note. She replied with a postcard collaged with the advice "Be glad of some little practical counsel." I framed it.*

I'm working on a few too many things at once, which is typical for me because I love saying yes to things even when it would be kinder to my future stressed-out self to say no. This month, I'm juggling a reported feature on mental health, a review of an author and film-maker, a profile of an actor, and a few smaller projects. But my long-term undertaking is a book about the Shakers, a utopian separatist religious group that was founded in the 1700s by a woman who believed in racial equality, the abolition of the nuclear family, a multiple-gendered god, and communalism. Initially, their primary form of worship was dancing, which they called laboring—their theory was that the body was the conduit for the divine. Equally, they were committed to work—and specifically mundane, anonymous labor—as a form of worship. Most people know Shakers because of their architecture and design (think Shaker cabinets or Shaker chairs). But the footprint of their theology, and their ideas about labor and creation and time and making the broken world more perfect through the work of your own hands, are so huge—so huge, and so fun and challenging to write about. That last bit, about a devotional practice of making the broken world more perfect, or letting yourself and your work be a conduit for that, resonates with me right now. ★

*Illustration by Kristian Hammerstad*

# RESURRECTOR

A ROTATING GUEST COLUMN IN WHICH WRITERS REEXAMINE CRITICALLY
UNACCLAIMED WORKS OF ART. IN THIS ISSUE: *AMERICAN PSYCHO* (THE BOOK)

*by Susan Steinberg*

**W**hen Bret Easton Ellis's *American Psycho* came out, I was working in a bookstore in Baltimore. I was just out of art school. My priorities were social. My state of mind was tragic. My intellect was a work in progress. None of this mattered then. Then, the word *wrong* meant "right." The books my friends and I liked were wrong. The music we liked was wrong. We thrived on our collective wrongness. I say this not as an excuse, but as a way to create setting. I wasn't a person who read reviews. I didn't know which works were unacclaimed. I still, more often than not, don't know. I mean, not unless it affects my life directly,

this woman would take her kid to see this movie. This had to do with religion. He shamed her so hard and so loudly, we had to leave. I cried all the way to the car. I thought we were in trouble. I thought we'd be punished by God. I worried our interest in a bad thing made us a bad thing. But on the ride home, my mother went off on the man in the vest. He was the bad one, not us. He was the one yelling, and fuck him. So there was the green light for me to determine my own spiritual corruption.

*American Psycho* was required reading when I was in grad school. This was years after its publication, and I was secretly intrigued. But my peers were upset that the book was required.

which *American Psycho* did. It wasn't because I read it, which, at the time, I hadn't. It was because it was controversial. This is an understatement. It was panned (and banned), and the local paper called the store to see if we carried the book. I'd been told to say we didn't carry any of the author's books. This was true. It wasn't about censorship but, evidently, taste. The books, it seemed, just weren't that good. I wouldn't share with the paper that I gravitated toward the tasteless. I also wouldn't share that I'd once read one of his other books and liked it. Instead, I'd align myself with the critics. And I'd rise, for the first time in my life, to that rarefied space of the virtuous.

I'm now remembering my mother taking me to see *Monty Python's Life of Brian*. We didn't know much about the movie going in, but my mother was a fan of Monty Python, and it was playing at the mall. There was a man in a vest tearing tickets in half. As we handed over our tickets, I could see he was angry. He was angry, it turned out, at my mother. He was outraged that

So the collective decision was not to read it. The collective decision was to skip class on the day we were to discuss it. It hadn't, though, occurred to me not to read a required book. By then I'd read so much required violence. Fiction was filled, so I'd discovered, with psychos. And I trusted our professor. He was curious, and now I, too, was curious. I wanted to know what was in this book so hated by those who hadn't read it. So I read it. I don't know how to describe what reading it was like. I'll just say it was startling. I felt stunned. Perhaps you wonder if this means I liked it. And I wonder: If I liked it, would you not like me? My opinion is, and always will be, irrelevant. So this isn't a recommendation. It isn't even a resurrection. I mean, the resurrection happened already. So it's more a recollection of one. It's more a gesture of one. It's more a *fuck you* to the man in the vest. Metaphorically. Literally. The story is: I went to class. Hardly anyone showed up. I still remember who did. ★

*Illustration by Kristian Hammerstad*

# THE ROUTINE: MADELEINE THIEN

## AN ANNOTATED RAMBLE THROUGH ONE ARTIST'S WORKDAY

**7–9 a.m.**

**7 a.m.**
Read the news in bed. Crushing.

**8 a.m.**
Read John Berger essay "The Chauvet Cave Painters." Felt grateful for all that Berger gave us.

*Thank you, John.*

**9 a.m.**
Coffee x 2. Only coffee has a regular schedule.

**10 a.m.–12 p.m.**

**10 a.m.**
Read Iman Mersal, *Traces of Enayat.*

**10:45 a.m.**
Sent edited novel to my editor. I started writing this novel in 2017! Momentous event. Dizzying. Ring the bells.

**12:16 p.m.**
Finished *Traces of Enayat.* Amazing. Wrote to Iman about book.

**1–3 p.m.**

**1:37 p.m.**
Wrote more emails. Hungry. Reheated lunch. Ate.

**2:30 p.m.**
Watered plants. One is dying; unsure why. Read the news.

*Lavender in the chill of winter.*

**3:30 p.m.**
Read Virginia Woolf + Wittgenstein's *Tractatus.* Prepped for teaching this week.

*Yes, that is a great slipper.*

**6–7:30 p.m.**

**6:30 p.m.**
Talked to my beloved, who is out of town.

**7 p.m.**
Cleaned. Cooked + ate while sending email. Watched *Taipei Story.*

*This dough rose for twenty-four hours in the fridge. A writer must be patient.*

**7:30 p.m.**
Drank wine. Tomorrow I must run or cycle. A little more work until bed.

**11:30 p.m.**

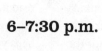

Zzzzzzz

8

*Pizza and coffee table photos by the author; John Berger photo by Ji-Elle*

# THE PROCESS

IN WHICH AN ARTIST DISCUSSES MAKING A PARTICULAR WORK

Kent Monkman, *They Knew Everything They Needed to Live*, 2022

There's no one like Kent Monkman. One can rarely say this literally *about fine artists*. Great paintings, of course, employ idiosyncratic vantages, styles, and metaphors, but their subjects and insights are seldom peerless. Yet Monkman—a Cree interdisciplinary artist raised in Winnipeg, Manitoba—and his historical, often fantastical paintings stand alone in the art world. His work responds to an education system bereft of Indigenous content, foiling this erasure using artistic, institutional, and commercial means. In so doing, he has become one of the only sources of the kind of cultural news he delivers.

Monkman not only fills a conspicuous knowledge gap for millennial Canadians like myself, as well as the generations preceding us, but does so with pointed ambiguity and figurative complexity. In 2019, he created two enormous paintings that subvert familiar narratives of colonial migration and its legacies, which were displayed in the Metropolitan Museum of Art's Great Hall. This drew me to Monkman's Being Legendary

9

*Acrylic on canvas, 54 × 72 in. Courtesy of the artist.*

*exhibition at the Royal Ontario Museum in spring 2023, where I stared for long stretches at various harrowing, playful, and ruminative works, linked by the odysseys of his gender-bending, time-traveling protagonist, Miss Chief Eagle Testickle.*

*"It's about giving people sensory experiences they can learn from instead of a fact sheet to read," Monkman told me when I visited his studio in Toronto's Eglinton West neighborhood to talk about* They Knew Everything They Needed to Live, *a painting from* Being Legendary. *He wheeled out the original for us to contemplate while discussing it. I confess I was so spellbound by its mix of realism and surrealism that more than once I had to forcefully redirect my attention to our conversation.*

—*Alessandro Tersigni*

THE BELIEVER: What really holds my gaze in *They Knew Everything They Needed to Live* is the juxtaposition of Louis Vuitton, stilettos, and rayon with traditional Indigenous life. The scene seems both historical and fantastical, which somehow makes it feel contemporary.

KENT MONKMAN: That aesthetic comes from the genesis of the character Miss Chief Eagle Testickle. I essentially created Miss Chief to reverse the gaze of nineteenth-century settler painters who made a lot of landscape paintings with Indigenous subjects—like Albert Bierstadt, George Catlin, and Paul Kane—by inserting her into their work. Her presence across time has a very contemporary perspective to it that had to be reflected through what she looked like. I decided she'd be drawn to Louis Vuitton. It's a French luxury brand that's been around since the time of the fur trade, so it fit perfectly. Blending contemporary and historical periods is a very Indigenous way of thinking, in many ways. It's the collapsing of past, present, and future into one time, which is all time.

BLVR: Does this painting itself have an origin story?

KM: This one is in reference to a knowledge keeper I know personally, Keith Goulet, who became a Cree linguist. It's not supposed to be Keith, but it's based on his story. He retained his language because he was never forced to go to residential school and grew up in the bush, where he learned how to hunt. Even as a child, he knew how to feed himself. Indigenous children had all this knowledge about how to live and exist here

that was given to them by their parents and grandparents. But it was lost in the settler school system, which brought a different way of teaching and different knowledge systems. *They Knew Everything They Needed to Live* is about learning from our elders. It's about this very expansive world that was shrunk throughout the colonial period by the extraction of children, which broke up those cycles of intergenerational knowledge. The painting has a tranquility, but that's a kind of premonition that something bad is going to happen. In the exhibition, the next painting you see depicts the Mounties capturing Indigenous children in a similar landscape. It's important to not skate over the fact that our world got smaller.

BLVR: I hesitate to ask you to concretize the artwork's symbols, but how do the petroglyphs and the little people fit into that?

KM: Because this work was shown at the Royal Ontario Museum, the exhibition was very much about comparing Western ways of looking at nature with Indigenous ways of thinking. For Miss Chief to fit into a Cree cosmology, she had to have relationships with other legendary beings. Almost all world cultures have mythical little people, whether they are leprechauns or a whole variety of others. We have stories of little people who are sneaky mischief-makers, known to live near the water's edge.

With the petroglyphs, the more I looked at them, the more they looked like dinosaurs. Rock drawings of thunderbirds looked more like pterodactyls to me than eagles. That hinted at the fact that, like our elders have always said, we've been here forever. Settler theories have generally estimated that Indigenous peoples arrived in North America around ten thousand years ago. While I was working on this show, I discovered the work of Cree-Métis archaeologist Paulette Steeves, who places Indigenous people on this continent roughly sixty thousand years ago to one hundred thousand years ago. That was mind-boggling to me.

BLVR: There's a geographic idiosyncrasy to this painting that's eloquent for me as a Canadian: wet lowlands, Carolinian forest, eastern white pines in the distance. Or maybe I'm projecting. Can you talk a bit about Canada as a milieu in your work?

KM: This to me is North America. The border is recent; it's pretty arbitrary. And so many Indigenous people would have moved around and across it. For foliage, often I'm looking at how other painters paint plants. For instance, these were all based on John James Audubon, an early-nineteenth-century North American botanical painter who painted a lot of birds and their environments. I wanted to have Western science and Indigenous cosmology collide in order to discuss the science that's embedded in our ways of knowing about all parts of nature, whether it's star knowledge or plant knowledge.

I don't really think about the painting as being Canadian, per se, but rather as depicting Indigenous land, whether it's what is now known as Canada or parts of the United States. It's really about challenging the myths of those two founding nations, which were designed to serve the settlers' purpose of occupying and dispossessing, and finding so many holes in them. Most North Americans haven't been taught these histories.

BLVR: Speaking of education, when I was at *Being Legendary*, I noticed the museum's two major Canadian galleries are closed indefinitely: the Eurocentric Sigmund Samuel Gallery of Canada and the Daphne Cockwell Gallery dedicated to First Peoples art and culture. Did that inform your curation?

KM: Basically, we got the First Peoples Gallery closed. That was part of the work. I do that kind of behind-the-scenes heavy lifting at museums. People refer to it as "decolonizing," which is one way of describing it. It's about undoing systems that have been set in place for so long that they're sedentary and continue to miseducate, misinform, and actually cause harm—particularly to Indigenous people, who encounter these authoritative voices telling stories about us that we had nothing to do with.

That was the case with the First Peoples Gallery. The problem is that museums can move very slowly, and you have these career-long bureaucrats who occupy very comfortable positions and are not challenged or forced to change the way things are done. I think there's so much value in museum culture and the way it communicates to society. You have to bring solutions that are going to move things forward in a joyful and positive way. No one wants to hear that kind of criticism unless you're able to give them something constructive.

These are all aspects of making paintings like this that people don't see. As an artist who's Indigenous, in addition to making art, I have to work hard to bring people to it. Having

default audiences is something that many artists take for granted. They don't have to deal with getting their audience to learn a whole bunch of new things just to enter the work.

BLVR: Does that mean that a viewer who doesn't do their own research or understand the historical context is a less ideal viewer for you?

KM: No, not at all. My goal is to make paintings that anyone can look at. Regardless of your age, background, or experience, there's going to be something for you. The layers will come for those who are interested in digging in to learn a little bit more. You'll have this beautiful, polished, seductive thing on the surface that pulls you in. Then as you start to peel back and work through those layers, you'll find more and more substance. I think if you can move people, emotionally or aesthetically, to learn, that's much more effective than getting them to read a news story. It's just the way we're hardwired to make connections.

BLVR: There are about a dozen people in the next room busily painting your work on canvases of all shapes and sizes. Clearly, your artistic practice is collaborative in some sense.

KM: It is collaborative, in a way. I've created this atelier model for my studio, based on how the old masters worked. As the master artist, I'm directing and conceiving of everything, but you also have to develop systems. It can be a collective process: from the kernel of the idea, through to the pencil sketches, to the reference photo shoots, to the smaller painted studies, and right up to the large finished works. It's all about training. I have senior painters that teach younger painters, and I have a painting manager. Paintings go into flowcharts. We have formal critiques in the studio at least twice a week. That's something I'm proud of. I've created an environment that's like a laboratory for experimentation, and trial and error.

BLVR: Does your team of painters have to learn how to manifest your style?

KM: Yes, and that very much became a way of transmitting how I want these paintings to be made. A lot of my painters were actually oil painters, so I've had to teach them my approach to acrylic. I use a lot of specific glazing techniques and very thin, transparent layers of paint. That's how the old masters could create so much depth in their color. I developed a similar technique with acrylic, the beauty of which is that, unlike with oil, those layers dry very fast. A great benefit of working with other painters is that it forces me to analyze what I do and communicate very subtle information about color and method.

BLVR: What about the concepts behind your work? Does your team have input on them? Is it an artistic collaboration as well as a practical one?

KM: It's really important to have the team informed as to what I'm about, so they can assist me in achieving the maximum effect. Most of the people I hire are artists in their own right and bring their creativity and expertise. I'm talking about the concepts all along, testing ideas on them, tweaking this, strengthening that, and determining if an idea is getting lost. My first audience is here in the studio.

For this series of paintings, we developed the exhibition with the Royal Ontario Museum, and I was in conversation with their curators and interpretive team, who were looking at my images and trying to wrap their heads around the big picture. I really relied on those museum professionals because that's what they do—they create these experiences for audiences. Through that process, we edited things, added some things, and filled in some gaps.

The point is that I'm never working in isolation. As an artist, I'm really interested in communicating. I know there is a certain kind of art-making that is a little more insular and self-reflective, but why would I want to talk only to a small audience or my own community? The whole purpose of putting all this energy out there is to reach the biggest audience possible.

BLVR: You're obviously the author of the work, the way a director is the author of a film. But I'm curious: Did you paint any of *They Knew Everything They Needed to Live*?

KM: Of course. I actually use that analogy of filmmakers or orchestral composers often. The best films are the ones where

the director doesn't have a heavy stylistic hand. They're just kind of barely there, and everything else is serving the ultimate purpose of that narrative. I feel like that's something I realized through maturing as an artist. I started as an abstract painter wanting to make my own unique mark with paint. I called it a wiggle. And I found my wiggle, but it becomes a very personal language that ends up leaving your audience outside the work. That's when I figured out that I wanted a more universal kind of language that reaches a wider audience and disappears my hand. The paintings I'm making in this studio with this team are as much me as anything I've ever made. Yes, I can do all these paintings myself. But we can make more paintings as a studio if we train more hands to make them. Also, paintings need time to evolve and unfold. Some paintings take years because you pause, reflect, innovate, and make discoveries along the way that you can't predict, because they happen by using the medium itself. Working with a team makes more time for all of that.

BLVR: Do you ever use yourself as a model? I get the feeling there's something of you in Miss Chief.

KM: Miss Chief definitely started out as me. I'm not always the body, but… I don't want to give away all my secrets! Face-wise, she's definitely me.

BLVR: How is your work received in the United States? Are Americans getting it?

KM: You know, they're about a generation behind, I would say, in terms of appreciating Indigenous contemporary art. But they're coming around. You can feel it happening. They've had so many other conversations there, about African American voices and Latino experiences, and the First People have somehow not been considered. I think that's a testimony to the effectiveness of the American mythology. They were so effective at removal and erasure that, in their minds, native people remained something from the past for a long time. But there are so many great museums in the States that are getting ready for new conversations. ✶

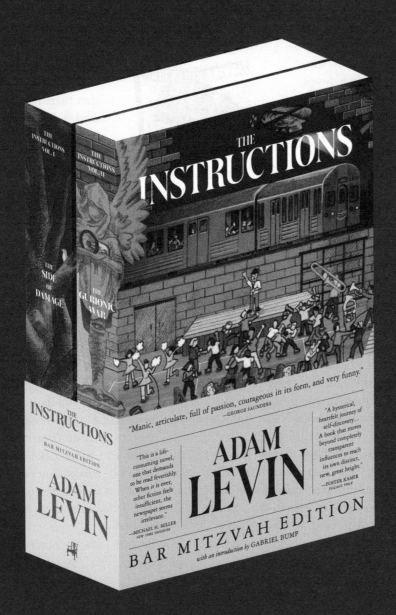

# HOW TO JOIN THE CULT OF ALTERNATE-SIDE PARKING

## A SERIES OF ESSENTIAL ADVICE

*by Lexi Kent-Monning*

**S**it in your car for eighty minutes twice a week. The street-sweeping window is ninety minutes, but if you arrive and leave on time, you're obeying New York City's Department of Transportation too strictly. Appease the city just enough. During the posted interval, the cars parked on the street sweeping side are parked illegally, but never change sides. Don't move for the street sweeper, either. To avoid a ticket, all you have to do is stay by your car. To join the cult, you must follow other rules too. And the social rules, the rules of the streets, are vast.

Be hyperaware but never look directly at anyone else engaged in the parking rigmarole. Not the boxing coach with a pit bull, the vintage-furniture dealer with a giant truck, the old ponytailed man wearing socks with sandals. If you have to talk to someone, never use the possessive when referring to their belongings. Never say "your dog" or "your truck"; rather, "that dog" and "that truck."

You'll be tempted to park by the twenty-four-hour bodega, which has security cameras and exterior lights that illuminate your car for all the hours you're not sitting in it. What you're forgetting about that presumed safety is the rats. They'll climb into your engine to nest, and when you turn the car on, the scent of rat piss will cloud through the vents. Instead, park halfway down the block—close enough to the lights and cameras to be included in their halo, far enough away that the rats stick to the bodega's garbage radius and leave your engine alone.

Don't work on your car during street-sweeping hours. Pop the hood, remove the nested leaves and rat shit, and spray the engine with rodent repellent only during off hours. Hotspot your cell phone to your laptop so you can work your job. Try to hide doing this, though, because it makes you look bougie. Typing is OK, but a Zoom call is out of the question.

Respect the hierarchy of the cult. In theory, everyone should be sitting in their cars for those eighty minutes. But in practice, there are the privileged few who no longer have to sit at all; they mill around a residential fence halfway down the block. Assume they were once like you, breathing recycled car air, and that there's a chance to be like them. The goal now is to graduate from car-sitter to fence-stander. The fence-standers include the bodega guys and the boxer, whose car is matte black and foundation-rattling loud. They stand at the fence and talk for the entire eighty minutes, never actually looking at or addressing one another, but taking turns monologuing without responding. This is their version of a conversation.

Enter the cult assertively but nondescriptly. Act like you've always been there. Emanate annoyance. Drive a forgettable beige car with no bumper stickers. Approach the fence-standers and comment on the dog—again, not "*your* dog," but "*that* dog." "That dog is a good girl." Don't look directly at the dog, either. Always rely on peripherals.

Leave room for hatchbacks to open their trunks. But don't make space for other cars to park. No, what we leave room for is people and their activities. The old man with the ponytail needs a three-and-a-half-foot clearance behind his Subaru. If you don't give him this territory, he'll call the city to give you a ticket even though you're parked legally. He'll lie and say you've been parked there for weeks when it's been only forty-eight hours. You've never seen him actually load anything, but the point is that he might want to someday.

Whenever possible, observe the ticket agent just as they are observing you. They also respect the hierarchy and don't ticket the fence-talkers, who don't have to sit in their cars like the rest of us, but do have to be near their cars. *The* cars. "The cars," not "their cars."

At the end of a six-month probationary period, you'll learn the pit bull's name. Pet her sideways instead of while facing her. Pretend you forgot something in your car so you can rub the dog's scent on it, hoping this might deter the rats. Most weeks, the street sweeper doesn't even come. That's irrelevant. Buy something at the bodega at the end of each shift. You're getting closer to leaning on that fence. ✭

*Illustration by Rich Tommaso*

# MARCUS THOMPSON II

[SPORTSWRITER]

"I WANT YOU TO FEEL WHAT I'M SAYING. I WANT THERE TO BE TURNS IN THE WAY YOU HEAR A CRAZY LINE, KNOW WHAT I'M SAYING?"

A few of the hip-hop artists that made Marcus Thompson II want to write:

*Too $hort and the Dangerous Crew*

*Goldy*

*Ant Banks*

*Ant Diddley Dog*

*Yukmouth*

*3X Krazy*

**S**portswriters are rarely heralded as cultural pillars. But Marcus Thompson II is—to use a sports term—a GOAT. A former beat writer for the Golden State Warriors and a current columnist for The Athletic, Thompson does what any memorable voice of their time does, regardless of genre: he observes deeply and speaks with a catharsis-inducing realness.

With a golden hand that produces as many as four stories a week, Thompson offers nuanced commentary and provides a rare human window into the fast-paced world of the NBA. One day he'll break the news of Steph Curry's players-only speech inside a locker room of defeated Warriors, and the next he'll explain how a single dunk may cause a tectonic shift in a franchise's roster management.

Even though Thompson has built a remarkable decades-long career, he wasn't born into the winners' circle. He grew up in deep East Oakland in the '80s and '90s and attended Oakland Tech. Early on, he memorized the East Bay's haphazard bus

*Illustration by Kristian Hammerstad*

system, riding three AC Transit lines across the city by swapping out bus passes with his friends—the same buses that locals like Too $hort began their careers rapping about.

As a teenager, he relocated to Georgia to attend the HBCU Clark Atlanta University. After writing for Atlanta Daily World and graduating with a degree in mass communications, he returned to the Bay and landed his first journalism gig in 1999, covering high school sports at the Contra Costa Times (now the East Bay Times). In 2001, he began cranking out stories about the basketball squad at Saint Mary's College of California, in Moraga, before eventually circling back to Oakland in 2004 to report on the struggling Warriors.

Today, the Warriors are seven-time NBA champions—and Thompson is one of the definitive sportswriters of his generation, having authored biographies of superstars like Steph Curry and Kevin Durant during Golden State's dynastic run. In the span of a fog-burned week, I chopped it up with Thompson on multiple phone calls while he was on the verge of finishing a big project about LeBron James during the NBA's free-agency period. I later ran into him at Chase Center before a Steph Curry buzzer-beating three-pointer sent us home in euphoria.

—Alan Chazaro

### I. THE SECOND LAYER

THE BELIEVER: As a fellow Bay Area writer, you're someone I've wanted to connect with for a minute. We're both in the middle of reporting stories right now, so thanks for taking the time.

MARCUS THOMPSON II: I appreciate that. We gotta represent one time for the Bay. You know Pendarvis Harshaw, right? That's my guy. I read everything he does.

BLVR: Yup. He's one of the ones. His writing, honestly, inspired me to leave my career as a high school teacher and pursue journalism. I saw what he was doing and was like, Damn. I want to do that, but with my Mexican American perspective.

MT: That's what's up. Being Mexican is one of the more undertold stories, especially in Oakland. I actually remember researching the Harlem of the West on Seventh Street. It used to be a Black neighborhood, but it was also a profound Mexican neighborhood for a while. That was why there

was Mexicali Rose and spots like that. It used to be mostly Mexican-owned spots, and people would just set up their shops all around there. Then they put the jail there, and you got the post office now, and the BART—that kind of changed things. But it used to be a thriving Mexican neighborhood at one point.

BLVR: That's wild. I had no idea and never knew about that history.

MT: Yes. When the railroads came west, the Bay Bridge was created to essentially hate on Oakland. It changed things. The ports were huge in San Francisco. But the [Central Pacific] railroad made the Port of Oakland even bigger and more important. The last stop on the railroad was West Oakland. So there was a whole new economy growing there. The ship conductors, workers, longshoremen—that was Black, Latino, working-class. They all had jobs. Then San Francisco built the bridge [in 1933] because they wanted that commerce.

BLVR: My parents immigrated to Scrillacon Valley in the late '80s, so I missed out on tons of local context like this.

MT: What did you say? Scrillacon Valley?

BLVR: Yeah. Most people call it Silicon Valley, but when I was growing up, the norteño rappers around there used to call it Scrillacon Valley. I say it jokingly. Kind of.

MT: That's what I thought you said. I remember the Luniz album *Operation Stackola*. The one where they're robbing a bank [on the cover]. At the top center it says "Scrilla National Bank." Great album.

BLVR: Definitely a classic. That gave us "I Got 5 on It." So what are you working on these days? I know it's the NBA offseason, but you always seem to be putting in work. I just heard you on an episode of *Hoops Adjacent* this week.

MT: *The Athletic* is actually doing a podcast on LeBron; it's this big series about his twenty years in this league. I got the Steph and LeBron episode. I had to write that today. I'm also writing about [Mike] Dunleavy becoming the GM [of the Golden State Warriors] and how gangsta his first move was.

Trading [Jordan] Poole? That was savage. I'm also trying to find out more about Draymond Green's situation. I don't think he's going anywhere. It's free agency, what we call silly season. You never know what to believe, and everyone has an agenda. I have a few more weeks before I take some time off, but I'm grinding till then.

BLVR: How did your career as a beat reporter start?

MT: I was covering Saint Mary's basketball in 2004 and Matt Steinmetz was the [Warriors] beat writer for the *Contra Costa Times* back then. I don't know what happened, but they asked me to write about Erick Dampier leaving the team. Steinmetz was off. I had pitched to write about the Warriors here and there, but it wasn't my job. Then they asked me again to write about Gilbert Arenas when he signed in Washington [DC]. I was like, *Hold up. This isn't my job.* I didn't know anything. I'm trying to call agents. The first piece was really hard. For the second piece they told me that if I wrote it, I'd become the beat writer. I wrote it, and a few weeks later, Steinmetz quit and I was the Warriors beat writer.

At the time, the Warriors weren't a big deal. There was a writer from *The Mercury* [*News*] and *The* [*San Francisco*] *Chronicle*, and me. I had no connections. I had nothing. I started from scratch. I didn't even know how to book road trips. I couldn't just ask my bosses, because it felt like proof that I didn't know what I was doing. Marc Spears was the one who helped me. I have to mention him. He was huge for me early in my career. He gave me phone numbers. Taught me how to book my trips. He had a map of where to stay in every city, how to rent cars, hotels near the arena that you could walk from, all of that. He was covering the Denver Nuggets at the time, and now he's at ESPN. Back then, salaries were hard to get information on, and you needed an agent to give you a salary sheet. The agents had it, but it wasn't common knowledge. I didn't know any agents. So Marc gave me a copy of that. Spreadsheets printed on paper about how much money players were making. I didn't know if I could do it. When I didn't have much help, Marc just came through. He's still that way. I would've failed, probably, if it wasn't for Marc.

BLVR: I can't imagine covering the NBA as a beat writer. It seems so competitive and hyper-paced.

MT: I've been doing it for so long, fortunately, so I can kind of survive without getting into all the other stuff. My contribution is my voice, more than anything else. Other writers can get the news. Woj [Adrian Wojnarowski] from ESPN, Shams [Charania], who's with us at *The Athletic*. They cover it all, regardless. They're gonna get it first. There was a point in my career when that's how we lived as reporters. That was the value of a reporter—just to break the news. But now, in today's landscape, I kind of live in the second layer. Someone will tell you what is happening. I'll tell you what it means and why it matters. I'd rather serve the people who read me in that way. It's healthier for my life. I did all that other stuff coming up in my career, so I get it.

BLVR: How was being a sports journalist different in the past compared with now? Pre-internet.

MT: When I started out, everything was in the newspaper. When you broke a scoop, you were king for a day. The competition couldn't do anything about it. That was your day. I'd walk into practice all swagged out. Nowadays, you got two minutes. You bust your butt and make all the calls and in many ways neglect things that matter to you, like family. You burn time and get information and maybe you're first and you got it and you're out there with it, and for a lot of us, that's worth about three minutes of pleasure. But the next person is right behind you. There's a lot of scorekeeping internally on who reported it first. I don't know how much readers care about that. In the end, you read who you read and follow who you follow. That's what it is. That game to me, playing that, is like eating crawfish. Lot of work for a little meat.

BLVR: I honestly can't stand crawfish.

MT: You need that special fork. All that for what? Give me some jumbo shrimp. You know how back in the day when you bought chips, and the bag was full with chips? Now it's like half-filled with air, less chips. That's like scoops today. Some are good at it, some aren't. For me, it feels like not enough chips are in the bag no more. I don't want to participate in that. I have a family. I don't want that anymore. It's like you skip dinner and then have to fix things with your wife later. I'll do the work, but my goal is to be more of a voice and provide fuller context rather than being the first person to tell you.

## II. A CRAB IN A BUCKET

BLVR: How did your time at Clark Atlanta University prepare you to become the kind of writer you are? When you left Oakland at a young age and slid over to the South, what did you gain from that pilgrimage?

MT: "I went from Oakland to Atlanta with my top down / $hort Dog, my shit is nationwide now." I was so eager to get up out of here when I left. All it did was make me appreciate where I'm from even more. It made me appreciate Oakland, the Bay, our culture, our lifestyle. Atlanta was great, but when I graduated, I only wanted to get up out of there. But still, when I left the Bay, I couldn't leave fast enough or get farther away than I did. Atlanta was way away. I told myself, I don't want to be able to walk back home to Oakland.

BLVR: Oakland was such a different place back then.

MT: Coming up, we didn't even have the outlets available like we do now. It was just rap, sell drugs, or if you're good enough to make it in sports, do that. Or, for some, go to college. That was a clear route for me. I wasn't a good athlete and I wasn't gonna sell drugs; that just wasn't me. College was my way. That's what I was taught and what I believe. Finish school, all that stuff. I knew that wherever I went, I just wanted to accomplish that and not be sucked back into the clutches of poverty and trauma. I understood back then what it was to be a crab in a bucket. If something happens, it pulls you back. I wanted to be far enough that it couldn't pull me back in.

BLVR: So why Atlanta?

MT: There was a girl in my neighborhood who went to Clark, who was a year ahead of me, and she told me to come. I remember being on the plane, flying to Atlanta, first time on a plane. You know how on the planes back then, they had basic screens that folded down for everyone to see? They would show a movie that everyone had to watch, and at the end they would show the map and you could see how far you'd traveled, the trajectory, flight path, all that. That's the first time I realized where Atlanta was on the map of America. The plane was approaching Georgia and it hit me. And I straight started crying, like, Yo, what have you done?

I'm by myself. I'm going to college. I don't know nothing. I've never been out of Oakland. I couldn't tell you how far three thousand miles was. Boy, I was straight crying.

But being in Atlanta and learning a different way of life, I just remember missing the Bay. Especially the diversity. At the time, Georgia wasn't particularly advanced. It wasn't even a sidewalk on every street, know what I'm saying? The stoplights were hanging from, like, a wire. It felt like the country with a *k*. Now it feels like a major metropolis, but in '95 it felt like the country. Even in the hoods of Oakland we had sidewalks and light poles. But I learned more about Atlanta as time went on, and the '96 Olympics changed a lot for Atlanta. I spent four years at Clark. A lot of people do a six- or seven-year plan.

BLVR: Atlanta has a reputation for a lively night scene. So it makes sense that people would want to stay longer. Just ask Lou Williams.

MT: Lemon Pepper Lou. Atlanta's definitely a problem, because it's hard to go to class. Once it's one o' clock [in the afternoon] and it's spring or summer, everyone's out. At an HBCU, it's all Black people, and we're kicking it like the festival at Lake Merritt [in Oakland] every day. I totally understood why some people didn't graduate on time. I even had to drop some classes and came back and finished at Laney [College, in Oakland]. At Clark, you'd see someone you know and stop and kick it on your way to class. I get how Atlanta will entice you not to finish.

BLVR: So you talked about wanting to get away from family at that point. I think many of us can relate. What was your family like, growing up?

MT: It was kind of a mess. I want to say it was a beautiful struggle, but it really wasn't that beautiful. My family was hit pretty hard by the crack epidemic. I grew up in Sobrante Park. I was nine when my parents split. I didn't know at the time what was going on, but it became clear that drugs were involved. Crack tore up our neighborhood. I'm talking the '80s. I was born in '77, so this is around '86, '87. I lived with my grandma, like everyone else did. Sobrante, that was the crack capital of Oakland. I remember trying to get girls to come over, and when they found out where it was, they weren't so sure about coming. It was super impoverished.

BLVR: That's pretty deep in East Oakland. It's incomprehensible to me how there can be such an aggressive disparity of wealth just a few miles from the Oakland Hills.

MT: There was a time when government assistance—you know, welfare—would come on the first and the fifteenth. Then I remember they switched it to only the first. That made it really hard for us. You had to make it last for a whole month. But have you ever asked an addict to do that? There was no re-up for them. Remember that Bone Thugs song?

BLVR: "Wake up, wake up, wake up / it's the first of the month…"

MT: Yeah. That's what it was like. There was just people getting shot, trying to stay alive. All that type of stuff. Lights out, water out. No phone. It was typical in that sense, but it didn't feel typical. Some people in our neighborhood had it better, and it felt like we had it worse, but come to find out as we got older, some had it worse than us. So it was time for me to get out of there. My dad didn't really get clean till I left for college. From the time I was nine till about eighteen, that was the worst of it. That's why I wanted to get out of there.

BLVR: How has the city changed since then? Do you ever go back to your old neighborhood?

MT: That neighborhood is mostly Mexican now, actually. Parts of Oakland are still dealing with major issues, but

they're not crack-related anymore. There's a huge wealth disparity in Oakland. That's a big issue. I live in West Oakland these days, still in the hood, but now I understand that there's two Oaklands. There are diverging pathways. I went to Oakland Tech and met cool people. You felt like they were rich compared to you. Even if they weren't. As a kid I didn't understand this other part of Oakland that existed. But now I'm really sensitive to it all. Cars get bipped and all that. I'm not for people robbing people, but I do sympathize. Hitting up cars to survive for a few days, that would've been us back then too. Oakland has become an epicenter of affluence. There are million-dollar homes out here. People are doing well, but the average rent is ridiculous. There are nice restaurants, but only some of us can access that lifestyle. There's still abjection that needs to be dealt with. In Oakland you can just go to the other side, where people are living much, much better than you. That's what happens when you have people living in depravity. I'm in a different place now. I have a job, cars, family, all that. But I can't forget about deep East Oakland.

### III. "I WANT TO TELL A STORY FOR YOU TO REMEMBER"

BLVR: Who are some writers that influenced you early on?

MT: To be honest, it really comes from hip-hop. Coming up, I read sports every day. *Sports Illustrated*, the local sports pages. There was a regular column in the *Chronicle* that my neighbor would leave for me at the house. But that column didn't make me want to write. Hip-hop did. I was enamored by the wordplay, the schema. Too $hort and the Dangerous Crew. I loved Goldy, Anthony Banks [Ant Banks], Ant Diddley Dog. They had a sophisticated level of how they rapped. At first, hip-hop was all East Coast. They were fast, creative, clever: Slick Rick, Big Daddy Kane, those guys. It wasn't no bubblegum rap. When it got to the West Coast I was even more enamored. I used to debate about it all the time with friends: Who's the best? That kind of thing.

BLVR: Who are some of your favorite rappers?

MT: In the '90s? Yukmouth. He was crazy. His storytelling and lyricism. There was no question who was better. Same with 3X [Krazy]. You know: Keak [da Sneak], Agerman,

B.A. They were lyricists. They were great. That drew me in and made me want to write. Then I went to school in Atlanta, so now you got André [3000]. He's crazy to me. That made my writing even better. I was a big Pac fan, too, since *Me Against the World*. That emotion, that power. I wasn't thinking about becoming a dope journalist. But I learned it all from what I listened to. In particular, hip-hop artists. I want you to feel what I'm saying. I want there to be turns in the way you hear a crazy line, know what I'm saying? I want to tell a story for you to remember. The way a verse starts and ends is extremely important. How do you start an article and end it? That also matters. I was indoctrinated by hip-hop, and it informs how I write, unintentionally. In hindsight it makes sense. And I was still reading Jim Murray, Gary Smith, Phil Taylor. When there was a Black writer in sports, people would point that out to me. Ralph Wiley. That

---

## THE WHITE-COLLAR DAY JOBS OF FICTIONAL SERIAL KILLERS

✴ Hannibal Lecter, psychiatrist
  (*The Silence of the Lambs* by Thomas Harris)
✴ Francis Dolarhyde, production chief of home
  movies division, Gateway Corp.
  (*Red Dragon* by Thomas Harris)
✴ Patrick Bateman, investment banker, Pierce & Pierce
  (*American Psycho* by Bret Easton Ellis)
✴ Gary Soneji, math and computer science
  teacher, Washington Day School
  (*Along Came a Spider* by James Patterson)
✴ Dexter Morgan, forensic blood splatter analyst, Miami-
  Dade Police Department
  (*Darkly Dreaming Dexter* by Jeff Lindsay)
✴ Norman Bates, proprietor of the Bates Motel
  (*Psycho* by Robert Bloch)
✴ Mathias Lund-Helgesen, doctor
  (*The Snowman* by Jo Nesbø)
✴ John Schuyler Moore, crime reporter, *The New York Times*
  (*The Alienist* by Caleb Carr)
✴ Louis Vullion, attorney
  (*Rules of Prey* by John Sandford)

—*list compiled by Gabe Boyd*

---

was cool, but I read that for information, for sports. I was a sports nut. I wanted to understand what was going on with the Warriors and the Bulls. But it didn't make me want to write. Ant Diddley Dog did.

BLVR: I'm embarrassed to admit I've never heard of Ant Diddley Dog.

MT: Bad N-Fluenz. That was a group in the '90s affiliated with Too $hort's label. They were a duo. Oakland dudes. At the time, it was heavy gangsta rap culture. Too $hort was hard bass, catchy lines, simple rhymes. That was his thing. And being vulgar, obviously. But Bad N-Fluenz were straight lyricists. They were hot and were about to blow up. Rappin' Ron was a freestyler. He would rap on the bus, shouting out people and their neighborhoods from the back of the bus, incorporating it all into his raps. And Ant Diddley Dog was a straight wordsmith. That just wasn't very common at that time [for Oakland rappers]. Fast, internal rhyme schemes. All that. They formed a duo and were affiliated with Too $hort's label. They were going crazy. That was way before the hyphy movement. 3X came after that. Agerman actually grew up a few houses away from me, matter of fact. They talked about crazy stuff in their music, but they knew how to rap.

BLVR: That's some real Oakland rap knowledge.

MT: That's how I grew up. I remember going to Atlanta, and it was very East Coast at the time. The South wasn't getting respect, either. That's when André said, "The South got something to say" at the Source Awards. That's around the time of *Southernplayalistic[adillacmuzik]*, *ATLiens*. It was predominantly Wu-Tang, *Hard Knock Life* from Jay-Z. But people would say the West couldn't rap. Cali was cool and deep but we didn't have the same weight as New York and all that. We had to defend ourselves. Most people only knew Too $hort, N.W.A, E-40, too, but he wasn't nationally respected like that at the time. So we played Yukmouth from the Luniz and Ant Diddley Dog to show them we could rap. Y'all think we can't rap in the Bay? Here, put this on. That was our argument. This was during the whole East versus West battle. Rappers helped us defend our culture. They were lyrical.

## IV. BROCCOLI AND BASKETBALL

BLVR: You've authored a few seminal biographies of NBA megastars like Stephen Curry and Kevin Durant. How do you approach writing about the life of an athlete, as opposed to a single game?

MT: Those books were two such different processes. They were both incredibly difficult, if I'm being real. There was a limit on access. The short story is this: I didn't even know how to do it, but I did it. You look back and you're like, Man, I really did that. For Steph, I had the benefit of having covered him his entire career. I got the book deal in 2016, when they went twenty-four to zero. I signed the book deal in January. But I'd already known him for so long that I didn't really need too much by way of access. The book was initially going to be about the Warriors season: seventy-three wins, historic year. All that. But things changed.

BLVR: Three to one. Three to one. I'll never forget those finals against Cleveland.

MT: Man. Once Kyrie [Irving] hit that shot, it changed everything. I had to switch up thousands of words.

BLVR: So you were working on the book during the whole season? Did you ever get to pick Steph's brain about any of it?

MT: Steph was a participant, but I didn't have to do any interviews with him about the book in particular. I could just ask my questions as a reporter. I was telling a story that wasn't over. We didn't know the end of it, because it was happening live. It's not like Steph was answering questions about the book while he was competing in the playoffs. They had a job, I had a job. It's so different, dramatically, from writing articles. My arrogance as a writer made me think I could just write all day, no problem. But I realized it's completely different. I had to learn how to write a book and not shorter articles. And they only gave me six months. They wanted it in July. I was ignorant and didn't know what it would be like. It turned out to be ridiculous. Eighty thousand words in six months of a constantly evolving story. I'm tracking the season and suddenly it's all gone, once they didn't win that title. I got maybe three weeks left. I'm in a Starbucks, trying to finish. Then the team signs KD. It was grueling, and I knew it wouldn't end. I went the route of penny-pinching questions throughout the course of the season, as I needed them. I also tracked down family, coaches, things like that. But I'd known Steph for many years, so I knew his story and was lucky in that aspect.

BLVR: How do you get NBA players to open up?

MT: To be honest, there aren't any shortcuts or tricks. The easiest way is the same way you get anyone to open up. Just treat them like people. They're individuals, so each approach isn't universal. You don't have to do much to get Draymond [Green] to open up. He just opens up. That's him. And once you put in the years and accrue that time, you know them and they know you. I try to be me, and whoever I am, if that vibes with them, I'm OK with that. If not, that's OK. There's a lot of people I don't vibe with. That's OK. Other media people with other personalities might get those people to open up and I might not. Some people require commonality; some people require rapport outside of basketball interviews; some people respect how you talk about the game. KD was like that. He enjoyed that: nerding out on basketball. But KD would also talk to me about broccoli. He just likes talking to people. Klay [Thompson] is cool, but he's different. He doesn't talk much. That's my guy, but he's just not a big talker. You have to understand that.

BLVR: I covered an NBA game this season and the press room was intense. Mind you, I'm not a sportswriter—I'm coming from the world of food and culture reporting—but it felt noticeably cutthroat. I had nothing to ask Jimmy Butler in a room full of reporters already asking him rapid-fire questions.

MT: My approach is to vibe with that intensity. I like to be contrarian and catch people off guard. Keep them on their toes, be funny. When I'm asking a question, I don't want a canned answer. Or I don't want them to be like, *Here go Marcus again*. Since they know me, I might go left or I might go right, and it's often based on inside jokes. It's different. That's built behind the scenes. It's easier to pull off when you've been doing it for a while. That Wardell situation, when I called [Steph Curry] Wardell? That was on the spot. They can't really see who we are. All they know is someone is talking, and you gotta be like, *Steph, over here*. I wanted to say something to let him know it was Marcus. It breaks the monotony. When I said "Wardell" he knew who it was. Steph still gives me a hard time for that sometimes. But I can throw it back at him.

BLVR: What do you think about the whole "old media" versus "new media" narrative? A few current and former players in the NBA, including Draymond, have been creating their own platforms and claiming that traditional journalists aren't worth their salt.

MT: I'm not really worrying about it. I don't think it's actually a problem between old media and new media. I think it's good media and bad media. That's the issue. I think it's hard to recognize from the players' perspective, because media is a varied field. Not all of us are on [ESPN's] *First Take*. Things that new media says they're doing are already being done by great journalists across the nation—but they're not usually the ones you see on TV.

When I was coming up, old media versus new media meant print or digital. The focus wasn't on how the media operated; it was about the technology shift. Old media had to turn in the story when the buzzer sounded, to make a print deadline. New media could be filing a story at 5 a.m. or later, because sometimes it doesn't really matter, depending on the story. You can develop a story after the buzzer and don't always have to rush it for the newspaper trucks. That was the dichotomy I remember with old and new media. But what players are talking about now is more the difference between bad and good media. They point out things that the media does poorly, which they're not wrong about. I consider myself new media because I write for digital platforms. I used to be old media on print platforms. When they say good media does *x, y, z*, I think I do that. I write about basketball, not drama—unless the drama noticeably impacts the basketball. We go to the sources and we ask what's up instead of lobbing shots from afar. I would argue there's plenty of people in this space doing good media. With honesty, with integrity, trying their best. But

they're just not on whatever show those players are watching and getting irritated by.

BLVR: Social media definitely doesn't help with that hysteria.

MT: Let's not act like the drama don't benefit everybody, though. Look, I have plenty of issues with the larger landscape of media. But the fans are very clear on what they want. You can write the greatest play breakdown of all time, but it don't hit like a rumor will. Know what I'm saying? We write so many articles a year. You can just look at the data. If you write a great analysis of a trade or someone's basketball abilities, you'll learn a lot from reading it. But then you write about a rumor, and fans make it very clear which one you should write more of. People like me, who are at a point in their career when they can take Ls, don't have to go viral. I'm not chasing those stories. I can take my time to write about assistant coaches and player profiles. That's my thing. But I can make that sacrifice. Part of media is giving people what they want. It's a catch-22. You gotta keep the lights on.

BLVR: OK, to wrap up here, do you have any advice for Oakland's youth, particularly those who might want to develop and share their voice, like you have?

MT: My advice is to know your worth. Your inherent worth, your accumulated worth, and your situational worth. It is likely greater than you suspect, than you imagine. If you understand your value, that should be your greatest pursuit—understand how immensely important and valuable you are. If you don't know it, others will dictate it to you. If you don't believe it, no one else will. Worth is not about finances, although you should understand what you're worth from that perspective as well. Your perspective has value. Your experience has value. Your talent has value. Your intangibles have value. Your beliefs have value. Your personality has value. Your dreams have value. Your being has value. ★

# ARRANGEMENTS

HOW ONE OF THE GREAT MASTERS OF THE AMERICAN SHORT STORY DECIDED, FOR THE FIRST TIME
IN HER LIFE, TO WRITE A COLLECTION OF RELATED STORIES

*by Ann Beattie*

A.

B.

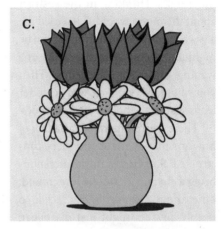

C.

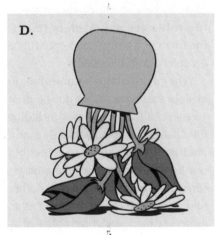

D.

E.

F.

**M**y grandmother's advice: after you've put on your jewelry, remove one piece. Similarly, there are those who approach flower arranging by plunging an enormous bouquet into a big vase—undoubtedly impressive—then pulling out the heavy-headed peony, or the show-stealing rose, along with all but one stem of fern. Maybe every stem.

Less is not necessarily more. A perfect arrangement of anything is subjective. You can turn the vase this way and that. Your inclination may be to vary the different flowers, or to separate them into several vases, but if you take the one-vase approach, you probably won't immerse the daisies in a clump, then group all the roses next to them. I know that some people hold the view that flower arrangements depend on the culture that inspired them, or admire or dislike the way flowers are presented because they express a new trend: obviously, the display sends one message when it looks one way, and carries different connotations when differently arranged.

When composing, certain short-story writers use the method of subtraction. I used to encourage beginning writers to make a messy rough draft, because when Flannery O'Connor wrote in one of her essays that you have to put something there before you can take it away, she meant exactly that: you

*Illustrations by Kristian Hammerstad*

have to *do* it before you can omit it. I go for rough-draft clutter because when I look at the typed word *moon*, that word might lead me to realize that there's a good reason to have my story begin in moonlight. Thinking in the abstract about the moon wouldn't have led me anywhere. What you don't need can be highlighted and deleted (the moon's waning, under your fingertips). Then you might ask yourself why a ladder leans against the house. And on it goes.

There are innumerable variations of how an individual story might be constructed. Sometimes those alterations bring a character into the foreground; other times, a character can recede so deeply, he/she might just disappear. (This was what my husband did in high school when he was forced to play softball: he'd be assigned to right field, where he'd slowly back into the woods behind the playing field, continuing to inch backward until he was obscured by the trees, then walk home.) Some of my characters have done the same thing to me, cleverly retreating. Others, who wouldn't shut up and always threatened to steal the show, got their way, even if I later deleted the whole story.

Writers have a love-hate relationship with characters who take on a life of their own. How will the writer prevail, amid scene-stealers? One obvious answer is: So what if you intended something? What might be gained, at least for a while, by following an uncertain path, an unknown plot?

I say this as Deep Background, and also to make quick remarks about a story's beginning, as opposed to my real subject, its end, after which comes (if the writer is lucky) a second ending: the story's placement in a book.

To varying degrees, writers wrestle with their characters, as the characters simultaneously wrestle one another. Sometimes it's as if a wrestling mat has been spread out, and the competitors have to work it out down there: the writer isn't even the referee; it's the writer who must adjust, not the characters. Similarly, as Raymond Carver wrote in his essay "Fires": "Somehow, when we weren't looking, the children had got into the driver's seat. As crazy as it sounds now, they held the reins, and the whip. We simply could not have anticipated anything like what was happening to us." This situation wasn't unique to the Carvers. They let the kids intimidate them because they felt overwhelmed, tired, or confused (psychologists give advice about how to deal with this dynamic all the time), but about the Carvers' children, I have to ask: Why should they behave better than fictional characters? Consider the number of times Carver admitted to being surprised by things that seemingly happened outside of his control in his writing. He quotes Flannery O'Connor, saying about her story "Good Country People" that "I didn't know there was going to be a PhD with a wooden leg in it. I merely found myself one morning writing a description of two women I knew something about, and before I realized it, I had equipped one of them with a daughter with a wooden leg. I brought in the Bible salesman, but… I didn't know he was going to steal that wooden leg until ten or twelve lines before he did it, but when I found out that this was what was going to happen, I realized that it was inevitable." Carver was relieved

to read this, because he thought it was his "secret" that he, too, composed this way. As many writers do. I'd say this is usual. Maybe not infallible as a writing method, but often the default position: in relinquishing power, the writer might gain a story.

But let's say that however the writer was overwhelmed, or left sitting comfortably, consulting notes for how the personalities and events in the story would emerge, ultimately a story came to exist, and if and when the writer was satisfied, there it was: it could continue on its trajectory into the world, sometimes in a magazine or literary quarterly, other times not, but held on to. What are writers to do with many of these successful stories, except aspire to give them continued life by collecting them in a book they hope will be accepted for publication?

The question then becomes how to arrange that book. What do you do if you have half a dozen stories, including one that's thorny and wickedly funny, another that has a golden center but is otherwise dreary, one whose narrator speaks tongue-in-cheek, another told from a dog's point of view? (As an aside: I remain particularly pleased by my story "The Debt," in which a dog who, as a puppy, was thrown out of a car window but lived, interrupts the present-day story to make remarks about its rescuer—a character who we already know is, in other matters, really a piece of work.) Back to what I was saying: I'm thinking that those hypothetical, dissimilar stories I've conjured up might be a first collection, unless the writer is a very protean writer indeed— though, to state the obvious, the majority of story collections are written by people who've attended an MFA program, so they might have understood their mandate from the first, about focusing on a theme or one character, whether they wanted to hear that or not.

In 2023, publishers want "related" stories. For example, ones with a consistent character who moves through them. Publishers also feel impelled to gain wider readership by labeling obviously related stories "A novel in stories." Or, in some cases, they simply assert that the tenuously connected stories constitute a novel. The novel is more than a reassuring touchstone; it's a kind of unmovable boulder, somewhat related to a concept the French have, which is to call memoirs novels. If your first book is a story collection rather than a novel, you'll be lucky—perhaps even so lucky that you have a two-book contract, and your stories are already written and the novel isn't, so that the stories are intended as your introduction as a writer, an early glimpse of your sensibility, as if writers are analogous to the lucky piece of turquoise a gambler touches for good luck before placing her bet. Or they're published because of overwhelming enthusiasm in spite of being stories, or for many other noble reasons.

Sometimes it will turn out that writers were wrong, and novels actually become their optimal genre. Other times, when a writer has written only one book, they can't be expected to know what they'll eventually write. I don't know if Grace Paley aspired to write a novel (or even if pressure was put on her to do so), but I never heard her say she did. (She never wrote a novel.) There are, of course, quite a few examples of short-story writers who've never published a novel, including one of the best short-story writers ever, Deborah Eisenberg. (Read "Twilight of the Superheroes." Why would she need to write a novel? This rhetorical question is also often asked about Alice Munro's transcendent late stories.) Raymond Carver never wrote a novel, even when his children were grown, and he had the money to eat, and he wasn't trying to write—of course, in longhand—during work breaks, sitting in his car, those times when he had a few moments off from janitorial work, or the sawmill. When he became very ill, he wished to exclusively write poetry. I knew the short-story writer Peter Taylor, who won the Pulitzer Prize for his short novel *A Summons to Memphis* (one of only three he ever wrote, over his long career). He was as bemused as he was appreciative, saying that "they" must have just wanted him to have it. He knew the genre on which his reputation justifiably rested.

I t's hard to generalize (and rarely helpful), but at least in first assembling one's stories as a collection, writers will probably stick to their original concept of how the reader should best come to know the characters: for example, James Joyce writing about people living in the small town of Dublin pre-1914. What troubles writers, it seems to me, is a question no different from one we consciously or unconsciously pose to ourselves that isn't restricted to writing: whether first impressions really are hugely important, even to the point of being indelible. We've learned from Malcolm Gladwell that people's impressions are formed frighteningly quickly, so, really, it might not be the best idea, if you're thinking about a logical order for your stories, to have an otherwise truly intriguing character kick things off by telling a stupid joke.

There's a kind of double burden in a story collection, because those who first appear, even when they become invisible later on, continue to tinge the stories that follow. So: think of your favorite short-story collection, and say which story comes first. Personally, I couldn't tell you this about any of my collections. I've certainly placed a story first with conviction, only to move it elsewhere, because, though I didn't want to omit it, it was wearing too much jewelry.

Who's to judge? The counterargument is that more can be better. My friend Liz wore forty silver bangles on her wrist. Janis Joplin never gave restraint a second thought. Though I've read *Dubliners* innumerable times, I don't remember which story comes first—or where stories are in anybody else's book. I can say which were my favorites, and I have that weird reader's ability to visualize where something is on a page, but not where in the book it's to be found. I'll know that a sentence by James Salter I want to read again (who wouldn't?) is on the right-hand page, two-thirds of the way down, near, but not exactly at, the end of a paragraph—but in which story? I can rarely zero in on it. I guess I do remember that Deborah Eisenberg's *Twilight of the Superheroes* begins with the title story, because I used to teach it, and I didn't have to flip through the pages to find it. (Some people demagnetize watches; my Post-it notes come unstuck.) "Midair" by Frank Conroy, from the book of the same title? Somewhere in there. It would be interesting to know where Alice Munro placed her title stories, those times when she had one, and if that varied by book. No doubt her editor Ann Close could say immediately, but I can't. I should also factor in that there are people who don't read from first to last. My brilliant friend Michael Silverblatt (of KCRW's *Bookworm*) once told me, in passing, that he first approached a book as a physical object; he'd hold it and think about it, then decide to read a bit of the last story, or even the book's final sentence (my god!), because getting a feel for the book was a way to enter into it. (He sometimes speaks reverentially about aspects of a book, from the typeface, to the paper, to the cover's embossed lettering—but it's just something he notes for himself. To Michael, a book is a tactile undertaking, as well as his opportunity to explore its contents.)

Since I'm so interested in how writers figure out an order in which to present their collections, why don't I retain that knowledge? I think, in part, because I'm a reader, definitely not of the Michael Silverblatt sort. (I'm too inhibited; he's at ease with books. He does a pas de deux with them, even when they're near strangers.) As for the title story becoming the book's title, I often agree with what the writer has separated out for special notice, but not always. Sometimes, although writers have the "right" title for an individual story (I used to happily let Roger Angell, or other friends, title my stories), one story's title is often not expansive enough to apply to the whole collection. As we all know, there's also marketing: it's not apocryphal that Grace Paley's *Enormous*

*Changes at the Last Minute* was often shelved in "Psychology." Such things are to be worried about.

In 1976, when my stories were first published as a book (*Distortions* contained nineteen stories, which by current standards is ridiculous), the collection didn't have to have a theme, and the stories didn't have to be related. I chose the ones I liked best, of the ones I'd written during the previous few years, and my agent submitted the book to publishers. Even then, they were pretty much the also-rans. I mean, I'd have—I was lucky to have—a two-book contract, and the other book *had* to be a novel (if you can believe it, there was a time, pre-memoir, and certainly no one had any reason to think I could write non-fiction then, including me). Rather than imposing a theme, all I had to do was some weeding, without any seeding. I like to think I was good at this—meaning, hard on myself. Certainly other people, in and outside of publishing, were an enormous help ("Oh, *that* story. Leave it out"). The order of the stories didn't have to do with a trajectory, or with the stories' interdependence: they were just there, like a box of chocolates: there was no *reason* the Madagascar vanilla buttercream should be next to the lemon verbena lavender-infused shortcake heart. There was likely to be a description of the chocolates inside the box (brilliant English majors are still often recruited for such jobs), so you could avoid eating a very delicate chocolate right after eating one with an intense chocolate taste that would overwhelm it, or you could simply try something and see if the

flavors clashed. Obviously, the candy descriptions had to be enticing, brief, and to the metaphoric point. While I suppose a similar little brochure could be included with a story collection ("Sweetly funny, with hints of salt and anomie"), short stories are already over-described. That's what reviewers do; they summarize them (at least in paraphrase; paraphrase makes everything strange), describing their inventive, unexpected, shocking plots. Books could come wrapped in paper, tied with ribbon, with cholesterol warnings rather than spoiler alerts… but enough. Sequestering

## ARTISTS AND WRITERS WHO WORKED FROM BED

★ Patricia Highsmith
★ Voltaire
★ Marcel Proust
★ Truman Capote
★ Louise Bourgeois
★ William Styron
★ Edith Sitwell
★ René Descartes
★ Vladimir Nabokov
★ Knut Hamsun
★ George Orwell
★ Edith Wharton
★ Mark Twain
★ Henri Matisse
★ Frida Kahlo
★ Virginia Woolf
★ Agatha Christie
★ James Joyce
★ Maya Angelou
★ Gioachino Rossini

—*list compiled by Bryce Woodcock*

during COVID was hard on me, as it was for many, many others.

That said, I've done something you won't be surprised to hear about. I've written a book containing six related stories. Let me qualify: related, but deliberately not interwoven. All the stories in *Onlookers* take place in the same Southern town, in approximately the same time, and involve characters who have a passing acquaintance with one another, or cross paths, but don't know one other well. They might live in the same building; a character might see the doctor of the first story exiting a food store (a real one) that my characters favor, but that's that. One character might visit another in a nursing home, but she'll be a relative's friend, not their own. I had fun going back into a story that had a short scene in which perfunctorily well-mannered middle-aged and elderly people eat together at a restaurant, and interjecting an opinionated, outspoken, though definitely not entirely wrong female doctor who is very upset and wants to stir things up. That happens in the first story in the book—I brought in a nonbeliever, an antagonist. Later, she appears in another story I'd written earlier, though I decided to place that story later in the book. In it, she's even angrier, provocative, and certainly not entirely wrong. She's a minor character, yet she speaks to an undercurrent in the first story that shakes up everything pleasantly banal that the characters have been agreeing about, exposing them, letting the reader know that someone is sounding an objection to life lived conveniently on the surface. You go, Bronwyn! What a pleasure to "develop" her in terms of a consistent trait (her big mouth), then later to place her in a situation that alters her life, so that while the anger remains a constant, it changes, and is there for a more personal reason.

When I began writing *Onlookers*, I wasn't thinking of a group of related stories. One of the stories was written nearly two years before the others, and the first and final stories were both written last, to bracket the book, once I realized what I'd been doing. (I admit: I sent it to my agent with eight, not six, stories. Her assistant, Mina, and she and her daughter Priscilla Gilman, who's also a writer and an amazing reader, independently felt that two of the stories should go. They were right—then the book was on track without two good stories that were also digressions. Thank you, Lynn, Mina, and Priscilla.) Also, the last story deliberately presents an inherent kind of digression, not only of character, but of milieu, though it turned out I was right about a previously mentioned minor character: he'd been waiting patiently for me to get to him. It had been my instinct that the final story should contain a different tone, rather than being smoothly incorporated into the collection. Energetic, too-talkative George could easily sustain it. Without him, that story's other character, Stacey, the empathetic head nurse where he works, could never have been revealed. It seemed to work to bring in the "wrong" character, in a collection focused on people and things that are never quite right for many different reasons. Loquacious yet rather inarticulate George became a different version of Bronwyn (whom he doesn't know; I couldn't have put those two together, because George operates on instinct, and would have walked out on her), yet Stacey's fondness for him, and what he provides her with, define her, and she's the one whose imagining ends the book. If she (if it) lifts off, it's all due to George.

There are many eminently sensible ways to end a book. When I asked Don Lee—whose shapely yet seemingly loosely held collection *The Partition* really impressed me—how and why he'd ended with the amazing three-story cycle, he gave me some background information: He'd written "The Sanno" as a stand-alone story, but because he'd flashed forward in it, he decided to write a second story about his character Alain ("Reenactments"). Then he realized he'd have to write a third: "I liked the idea of covering one character's life over forty-five years, especially as a parallel to the title novella in my first collection, *Yellow*, which had followed a character from adolescence to middle age. With both collections, it made sense to me to end with the longest piece of the cycle. Otherwise you run the risk of alienating readers if they aren't drawn to the long work, whereas if you begin with some unrelated stories, they can quickly turn to the next story if the first doesn't grab them." (This, from a person who worked as a brilliant story editor, as well as being a writer. I'd say that Don has a heightened awareness about how many readers read story collections.)

As for my late friend Peter Taylor, he was asked in 1987 (the year he won the Pulitzer) how he'd like to be remembered. Answer: "I would like to have as many of my stories as possible survive and be read and liked." Maybe it went without saying that now people would take note of his having won the Pulitzer, but I think he meant what he said: read the stories, please. (He took a little distance from himself as he continued: "At my age it's hard not to want to feel that your last book is your best book.")

Maybe where a writer ends a collection depends on their temperament, as well. Joyce knew, after he'd written *Dubliners*, that the book needed one more story to complete it, and he made it a difficult one, a far-reaching story that was obviously rooted in things he wanted to say about Dublin (and Ireland). "The Dead" became the final exploration, and the ultimate purpose, of the book. It also happens to be the most magnificent story. (Elsewhere, he wasn't going for magnificence.) I don't think he was so much pulling out all the stops as making the reader pause to see that he knew them. It's a story that makes you rethink all the others, which is a hard thing to do. In many story collections I admire—whether the heartstopping story comes first, last, or in the middle—the ordering has been thought out, even if it misfires. If there's a *Collected Stories*, writers do have a chance to take the obvious approach, and reprint them chronologically (which might take into consideration when they were written, rather than when they were published). I think writers are very aware of how they've changed; it's just that they might have doubts about whether that change is necessarily good—as Peter Taylor hints. But with a first collection being published now, well: if the stories are mix-and-match, the writer will probably either not get published, or will have to make concessions. Is it depressing or painfully consoling that the publication of *Dubliners* was delayed by Grant Richards, the London publisher, for seven or eight years because of concerns about how certain things Joyce included might be upsetting to Dublin's inhabitants? (Imagine *Dubliners* with trigger warnings.)

*Onlookers* is my ninth collection (tenth, if you count *The New Yorker Stories*), but I caved: *related stories*. Though it wasn't as painful as I thought, because the book's variations on a theme snuck up on me, somewhat the same way Don Lee's first Alain story led him onward to the others: my six stories involve the taking down of Charlottesville, Virginia's Confederate statues, though I didn't write about a rally I didn't attend (I'd moved). What I did try to address was the covert or unmeasurable effect this debate—and of course the horrifying rally of August 2017—had on different characters during a similar time period. In some stories, the statues are still in place; in others they're gone. As I wrote, some of them truly disappeared overnight; I have photographs of others in various stages preceding their exit, with graffiti sprayed on their bases, or plastic netting barriers built around them. And, along with Robert E. Lee sitting atop Traveller, the monuments vary: also removed was a statue of Lewis and Clark with Sacagawea, a subject that's revisited from story to story. Regardless of differing opinions, it was deemed necessary to get rid of the towering male explorers and the subservient woman over whom they tower, while other characters explain in a vexed way that *of course* she was kneeling: she was a guide! A guide would look at tracks. Nevertheless, the debate and the solution regarding the highly contested statues became a constant refrain. These issues were there, even when they weren't talked about, even when Bronwyn wasn't raging. COVID, too, got into the book because there it suddenly was, a reality. Nothing I'd set up had been quickly or easily solved (if it is, why write?), but I kept feeling that one additional perspective—a personal vision—was needed. I think that would have gotten lost if I'd placed it earlier. But it's certainly a different book if, because of its length, the reader doesn't read the final story. It's the reader's loss if they have the same attitude about the Alain stories that end Don Lee's book, and it's just unthinkable that someone might pick up *Dubliners* and stop after reading the next-to-last story, and think, I get it. That's enough.

Read to the end, please! Ask yourself why the writer chose to end on that note rather than another. Then reconsider the collection from the writer's perspective as well as your own. If the writer's guessed right, you can feel their presence hovering, taking a motionless bow, silently speaking to the work's subtext, maybe, or even turning a little mean, provocative. Writers can keep themselves out of a book for only so long, and the final words of their final story often give a huge hint about what was at stake all along. Of course, as is true of "The Dead," whatever you read is likely to be O so eloquently expressed—one final revelation, one final wager. ★

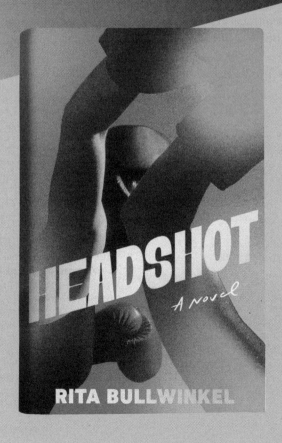

# CLOSE READ

UNPACKING ONE REDOUBTABLE PASSAGE. IN THIS ISSUE: AN EXCERPT FROM "ACTIN CYTOSKELETON AND COMPLEX CELL ARCHITECTURE IN AN ASGARD ARCHAEON" BY THIAGO RODRIGUES-OLIVEIRA, ET AL.

*by Veronique Greenwood*

"Asgard archaea are considered to be the closest known relatives of eukaryotes. Their genomes contain hundreds of eukaryotic signature proteins (ESPs), which inspired hypotheses on the evolution of the eukaryotic cell. A role of ESPs in the formation of an elaborate cytoskeleton and complex cellular structures has been postulated, but never visualized…

"Considering that lokiarchaeal organisms and other Asgard archaea can be found in a variety of anoxic and often marine environments, we screened DNA from shallow-water sediment from different locations for the presence of 16S rRNA genes of Asgard archaea to select suitable and easily reachable sampling sites for establishing enrichments. Sediments from a small estuarine canal that regularly receives water from the Mediterranean near the coast of Piran, Slovenia, were identified to have the highest relative abundance at the 13–16 cm depth layer, exhibiting up to 4% of Asgard archaea 16S rRNA genes in amplicon sequencing...

"With periodic monitoring using quantitative PCR (qPCR) with Lokiarchaea-specific primers, growth could be observed after 140 days at 20 °C in serum flasks containing sterile-filtered water from the original source supplemented with complex organics (casein hydrolysate, milk powder and amino acids). However, after two transfers under these conditions, growth could no longer be detected and a second round of screening with different medium compositions was performed. Using a modification of the medium MK-D1 reported for the cultivation of 'Ca. P. syntrophicum,' cell growth recovered, and abundances reached repeatedly 2–8%. However, higher enrichments were not achieved under these conditions. Only through developing a minimal medium, mostly by reducing the input of organic carbon sources to a single compound and by increasing antibiotic concentrations, lokiarchaeal relative abundances reached between 25% and 80% after several transfers.…"

---

Thirteen years ago, microbiologist Christa Schleper and her coworkers hauled a tube of mud from the floor of the North Sea. In it they discovered a group of microbes that could tell us about the origins of our branch in the tree of life. Now they've finally managed to grow enough in the lab that they can look at them under a microscope. Here's how—and why—they did that.

1. First, the basics: You are a eukaryote. So is everything whose cells have a nucleus and mitochondria. Bacteria are not; they're prokaryotes, and somewhere way back, it was a prokaryote that evolved and changed and became the first eukaryote. Mitochondria are the remnants of a

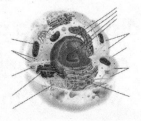

long-ago bacterium that was somehow subsumed by early eukaryotes. Archaea are neither bacteria nor eukaryotes. They are microbes, but aspects of their cells seem to be like ours. That's especially true of the Asgard archaea, the ones Schleper and her colleagues detected for the first time in that North Sea mud.

2. Important note: Asgards' genomes, which you can fish out

of the mud without culturing a living organism, are almost the only thing researchers have been able to study so far. These bugs are wildly finicky about their living situation: they are the hothouse orchids of the microbial world.

3. These are genes that we thought only eukaryotes had, things that make us special. Until the Asgards came on the radar.

4. That is to say: Are they a peek into what our earliest eukaryotic ancestors might have looked like?

5. Some of these genes code for a protein that looks like actin, the building block of a kind of scaffolding inside your cells. Are Asgards structuring their cells like we do?

6. An understatement! Before this paper, the only time anyone had actually seen an Asgard archaeon was after a Japanese group spent twelve years culturing enough of them to photograph. They got only a few snapshots, and they didn't get to do experiments with the cells before the cells died.

7. They looked in a lot of places for some nice high-quality mud.

"Amplicon sequencing analyses of 16S rRNA genes revealed that the culture with the highest enrichment (Loki-B35) consisted of three dominant and two minor species: a single Lokiarchaeon sequence (79%), a sulfate-reducing bacterium of the *Desulfovibrio* genus (10%), a hydrogenotrophic methanogen of the *Methanogenium* lineage (6%), as well as a *Halodesulfovibrio* and a member of the *Methanofastidiosales* genus (both at around 2%)....

"We next plunge-froze cells of a live culture onto electron microscopy (EM) grids to image them in a near-native state using cryo-electron tomography (cryo-ET).... This approach revealed three general cell types that had distinct morphologies and cell envelope architectures. One class consisted of round-shaped cell bodies associated with elaborate and heterogeneous protrusions. The other two cell types were rods and spherically shaped cells, respectively, without protrusions. Their cell envelopes had canonical Gram-negative and archaeal cell envelope features, therefore probably representing co-cultured bacteria and archaea. By contrast, the cell envelope of '*Ca*. L. ossiferum' candidates featured complex unordered densities protruding from a single membrane....

"Having established the identity and general appearance of '*Ca*. L. ossiferum' cells, we next aimed to analyse their overall organization by scanning EM. We identified small coccoid cells with surface-bound vesicles and extensive protrusions. In contrast to '*Ca*. P. syntrophicum,' these long protrusions appeared more irregular, frequently branching or expanding into bulbous structures...

"We discovered an elaborate actin-based cytoskeleton in Asgard archaea, which has long been hypothesized, but has not been visualized...

"The elaborate cell architecture with extensive membranous protrusions has multiple implications for Asgard physiology and ecology. As these characteristic features make the cells highly fragile, it could also explain why the highest abundance of Asgard archaea is found in sediments rather than in plankton....

"The large surface area of the convoluted network of protrusions, in combination with the unusual cell envelope lacking a highly ordered S-layer (as typically found in other archaea) but rather displaying numerous surface proteins, may have enabled the intricate cell–cell contacts required for eukaryogenesis that—considering the lifestyle of the two cultured Asgard strains—probably involved interspecies dependencies in syntrophic relationships. These findings strongly support a gradual path of mitochondrial acquisition through protrusion-mediated cell–cell interactions." ★

---

8. This Slovenian ditch had the highest density of Asgard archaea of anywhere they looked. If you're going to grow them in the lab and have enough to do experiments with, you have to start with an Asgard-heavy sample.

9. Four percent doesn't sound like much, but that's a lot of Asgard archaea in one place!

10. They're growing! Exciting!

11. They stopped growing. Sigh.

12. It took months and months of trying lots of different things for the scientists to get these Asgards—a type known as Lokiarchaea—to grow well. They were trying various tricks that the Japanese group had used, which included Japanese baby formula.

13. Before they tried to look at the cells, they did DNA testing to see what exactly had survived.

14. What they found: these Asgards grow best when they have some bacterial friends living with them. The researchers think these bacteria may be producing molecules that Asgards can eat, providing a kind of neighborly buffet.

15. To take a look at the cells, they froze the Asgards and their bacterial friends, slivered them like fine pastrami, then bounced rays of electrons off them. This produces crisp images of the cells' silhouettes.

16. These are the Asgards.

17. These are the bacteria.

18. My new band name. Also, a way of saying that these archaea are funny-looking.

19. Once they finally got to see the archaea, they were wildly odd. They had snaky arms, little tentacles, strange blobby bits.

20. What's more, the scientists were able to confirm that the Asgard cells had something forming threads within them, like the actin in your cells, confirming their strange synchrony with eukaryotes.

21. These wiggly bits are very delicate, helping to explain why, until Schleper and her colleagues pulled up their North Sea mud, nobody had noticed Asgards living all around us in the soil—touch them and they fall apart.

22. And here, folks, is the mic drop: If Asgards have long limbs that they can drape over their generous bacterial neighbors, could it be that we're seeing something like what happened when early eukaryotes picked up the bacterium that became the mitochondrion? Did early eukaryotes extend a protrusion and start a chain of events that led to you, here, now, reading this page? ★

# LOVE & MURDER

On Rian Malan's 1990 memoir, My Traitor's Heart, *and what it mean*

# N SOUTH AFRICA

*e a tourist in your own country.*  by **EULA BISS**

OPENING ILLUSTRATION BY:
*Kristian Hammerstad*

PHOTOGRAPHS THROUGHOUT BY:
*the author*

**M**y first encounter with South Africa was a book, *My Traitor's Heart*, which I read when I was twenty, and it was because of this book that I traveled to South Africa twenty years later. I don't know where I thought I was going then, but it might have been further into the book, which was a reckoning with what it means to be white. The author, Rian Malan, is a white South African who worked as a crime reporter during the death throes of apartheid, and he told the story of his country through a series of murders.

South Africa had the world's second-highest murder rate in 1990, when *My Traitor's Heart* was published. Those were the days of burning tire necklaces and cursory executions. Murder in apartheid-era South Africa wasn't like murder in other countries, according to Malan. "Elsewhere in the world, murder was just another function of ordinary social relationships,"

he observed. "In the vast majority of cases, murderers killed someone they knew—wives, bosses, fellow drunkards, rivals in business or love. In South Africa, it wasn't like that. In South Africa, you could be walking down the street, minding your own business, when white trash boiled off the back of a passing pick-up and kicked your head in, simply because your skin was black." Re-reading that passage on the plane to Johannesburg, I could think of at least one other country where murder was like that, the only country I really knew. But when I read *My Traitor's Heart* at twenty, it wasn't the murders I recognized—it was the psychological state of the author.

He was disturbed by his country and confused about his place in it. He had grown up in a middle-class suburb of Johannesburg, where he saw very little of the violence that enforced apartheid. But he read the news, and he wondered who he was. His people, in South African terms, were Afrikaners, an ethnic group descended from Dutch colonists. "The white tribe of Africa" is how Malan described Afrikaners, "arrogant, xenophobic, and 'full of blood,' as the Zulus say of tyrants." His family, the Malans, had been in South Africa since 1688. A Malan died in a massacre of Afrikaners by King Dingane ka Senzangakhona's Zulu warriors, and the brother of that Malan massacred Zulus. A Malan fought in the first war against the British, and a Malan died in the second war against the British, the war in which Afrikaners were held in concentration camps.

There was one Malan buried in the archives who haunted Rian Malan more

than the others. This Dawid Malan was the master, until 1788, of the finest estate in the Cape Colony. He owned slaves and vast vineyards, which he abandoned to run away with his neighbor's slave, a black woman named Sara. Taking nothing with them but two horses, Dawid and Sara disappeared from the colony and the historical record. Sara never reappeared on paper, but Dawid resurfaced several decades later, on trial for violently defending an Afrikaner's right to beat his black servant. "The man who abandoned his birthright for the love of a black woman had become what would one day be called a white supremacist," Malan wrote, "willing to die rather than accord black people equality before the law."

More than a century later, in 1948, another Malan, Daniel François Malan, led the Afrikaner nationalists to power on the promise of a "final solution." This was apartheid, a gridlock of laws that divided the population into racial groups and intervened in every aspect of life, from sex and marriage to work, housing, and education. Apartheid eliminated mixed neighborhoods, mandated segregation, and separated families. A byzantine system, the Pass Laws, controlled the movement of black South Africans within the country, and hundreds of thousands of black people were arrested each year for violations of these laws.

The young Rian Malan opposed apartheid, but not in any way that he would later consider meaningful. "We believed that apartheid was stupid and vicious," he wrote of himself and his teenage friends, "but we also believed that growing our hair long undermined it." He and his friends spray-painted SAY IT LOUD, I'M BLACK & I'M PROUD

in six-foot letters on an embankment in their suburb, and Malan showed a photo to his family's black maid. Her response: "Ah, *suka*." Get lost. Malan had never heard the James Brown song, but he'd read about it in *Time*. He knew more about American culture than he knew about the culture of the people who lived in his backyard, in shacks. "The strangest thing about my African childhood," he wrote, "is that it wasn't really African at all." Malan was more Western than he was African—because he was, more than anything, a product of apartheid.

At twenty, I recognized myself in the young Malan. I saw my own undeveloped politics, my own failings and my own frustrations, my own crisis of conscience. I saw the deficiencies in my education, which was, in many ways, an apartheid education. I had been fed mostly platitudes about race in America and I was hungry for real talk, so I was drawn to Malan's impatience with empty gestures and his intolerance of pious pronouncements.

At forty, when I traveled across South Africa carrying *My Traitor's Heart*, I read the book at more of a remove. I saw how often Malan describes black Africans as unknowable and inscrutable, with customs and conflicts that could never be comprehended, and of Africa itself as unfathomable and otherworldly. He compares white South Africa to a moon base, by which he means that it was insular and artificially maintained. But outside that base, in the townships and homelands of black South Africa, everything is alien to him. His book is the artifact of a mind still half-entrenched in apartheid.

The young Malan believed that he loved the black people in his life, the gardener Piet and the maid Miriam, who raised him. "Maybe it was the love of a prince for his loyal subjects," he later recognized, "and conditional on their remaining loyal and subservient." In high school he broke apartheid law when he slept with a black woman, but he didn't know her name, and his most frequent contact with his black compatriots was when he bought dope. "I yearned for black friends," he wrote, "…and in the end I was given some." These were his colleagues at a progressive newspaper.

Malan was working as a reporter for Johannesburg's *Star* in 1976, the year of the student uprising in the neighboring township of Soweto. On June 16, twenty thousand students walked out of the schools to protest apartheid, and were met by the police, who fired tear gas and live ammunition, killing hundreds of children. The next day, helicopters and armored cars were called into Soweto, but the uprising continued, and spread. White South Africa was on edge. "Whenever my telephone rang, some white paranoiac came on the line to pass along another rumor," Malan recalled. Someone had heard that tomorrow was kill-a-white day, for instance, or that black maids had been told to poison their employers' tea. While the black people of Soweto were mourning their children, the white people of Johannesburg were preoccupied with fears of imagined vengeance. In the midst of this paranoia, Malan answered a call reporting a real act of vengeance, a black man shouting, "Africa! Africa!" and swinging an axe at whites on the streets of Johannesburg.

Malan's first thought was that if he himself had been in that axman's path, all the good he'd ever done would not have saved him. He had disdain for the white paranoiacs, but he shared with them a fear that he was not safe. Fear, as he came to understand, was "the force that held the white tribe together." He sympathized with the axman's cause, but still, he didn't want to be killed. He wanted to be seen and recognized for who he was. He wanted, in other words, to be loved. He wanted this for all the reasons people want to be loved, but for another reason, too, a reason intimately tied to his race—he wanted proof that he was good, because he knew the system he was embedded within was bad.

I have to wonder now why I keep returning to this book. Beyond the spectacle of the murders—beyond the melodrama of Malan's tortured relationship with his country, beyond the unanswerable question of what it means to be white—is a problem that continues to captivate me: the problem of love under apartheid, which is now the problem of love in the ruins of apartheid.

The emotional landscape of *My Traitor's Heart* was so familiar to me at twenty, that when I boarded a plane at forty, I was still under the impression that I was going somewhere familiar. I was disabused of that notion even before I left the airport in Johannesburg. Dizzy with sleeplessness, I stood before a sign on the bathroom door and wondered what it meant. The sign was wordless, like the falling figure that indicates a wet floor, but it was communicating something else, in a universal visual language I did not understand. The sign was a reminder that I was not well traveled. Of the eleven official languages of South Africa, I spoke only one. This was an expansive country of wide velds and high deserts, mountain ranges and coastline, surrounded by three oceans, with a history that stretched back to the very beginning of humankind, and I knew next to nothing about it.

I stepped into the city feeling chastened. Flowers I couldn't name poured over brightly painted fences topped with razor wire. That first evening, I walked the streets of Johannesburg with Glen Retief, a white South African writer. He was the only South African I knew, and I didn't know him well—not well enough to have asked him to bring me along when he traveled back to his country from the United States. But here we were, both of us stopping and turning when we reached the edges of the neighborhoods that were familiar to him. If Glen was an imperfect guide to a country where less than 10 percent of the population was white, I was a more imperfect student. I had arrived with an independent study in mind, but I was doubting the whole endeavor already. I'd made a mistake, I confessed. It was crazy of me to have thought that by going to Africa I was somehow going deeper into my own country, into a place that would help me understand the place I came from. Glen, who had been living in the United States for most of his adult life, did not think this was crazy. What the United States and South Africa have in common, he said, is that they are both postapartheid states.

WELCOME HOME read a sign at the entrance to the Apartheid Museum. The museum was located between the city center of Johannesburg, which had been designated a white area under apartheid, and Soweto, the township that became, under apartheid, the largest black city in South Africa. The surrounding landscape was scrubby and arid, scarred by mining. This place was home, in that human life first evolved here, with all humans sharing one common ancestor, a woman who lived hundreds of thousands of years ago in what is now South Africa.

The museum was packed with schoolchildren, each group in matching uniforms, entirely purple, from the slacks to the shirts; or entirely blue; or entirely red. They were a beautiful sight, these children, streaming around us in their bright colors with their excited chatter. They were all black and all "born free," as they say in South Africa—born after the first democratic election that marked the end of apartheid, in 1994. Glen was moving quickly through an exhibit of anti-apartheid posters, looking for one that he might have pasted on a wall himself, but he stopped abruptly at the sight of a heavily armored vehicle topped by a machine gun and surrounded by a crowd of children. It was a sight that called to mind the Soweto Uprising, the children fired on by the police, and the armored cars that had rolled into Soweto the next day.

This armored car was a Casspir, which the police used to patrol the townships of black South Africa in the final decades of apartheid. Later, South Africa sold Casspirs to the United States, which used them in Iraq and Afghanistan, and in the War on Drugs, a war on our own people. In 2014, a Casspir, or one of its cousins, showed up at the protests in Ferguson, Missouri.

This Casspir emanated a metallic scent of use as we climbed through the narrow door. The interior was dark, with small windows, one cracked. Probably by a rock, Glen said. Rocks were the weapons with which the children of the townships fought the police, in uprising after uprising. Rocks and bricks and Molotov cocktails. This vehicle would have been manned by white boys just out of high school, afraid and unprepared, doing their mandatory military service. Glen had refused that service, and left the country in his twenties. Now he lingered inside the Casspir and said quietly, "Imagine being one of those boys." This armored car was like white South Africa, he told me— a confined space that was heavily protected, a psychological prison, but a safe one.

There were 131 nooses hanging from the ceiling of a small room just beyond the Casspir. When I saw them through the doorway, I felt dislocated, as if they had followed me there, as if lynching were in the air I carried. Each noose represented the execution of a political prisoner who had been sentenced to death by hanging. The list of names on the wall did not include those who were killed without having been tried and sentenced, so it did not include the name Bantu Stephen Biko.

Biko was a leader of the Black Consciousness Movement, which emerged in the silence following the Sharpeville massacre of 1960. Informed by a diaspora of thinkers, from W.E.B. Du Bois and Marcus Garvey to Aimé Césaire and Frantz Fanon, Biko was a philosopher of the psychic impact of apartheid. "Not only have they kicked the black," he wrote of the Afrikaner nationalist government, "but they have also told him how to react to the kick." Refusing to cower before the kick was the foundation of Biko's philosophy. Black Consciousness, as he saw it, was not a means to an end. It was an end in and of itself—to live with dignity. "The most potent weapon in the hands of the oppressor," he wrote, "is the mind of the oppressed." And so to be "conscientized" was to reclaim your own mind.

From Johannesburg we flew to Port Elizabeth (now Gqeberha), where Biko had been imprisoned before his death. There we began driving across the Eastern Cape province into one of South Africa's former "homelands." These were reservations designated for native Africans, who could obtain passes to work in white South Africa but could not live there. "Sophisticated concentration camps" is what Biko called the homelands, where 80 percent of the nation's people were forced onto 13 percent of the land. Over three decades, 3.5 million people were relocated to the homelands, one of the largest mass removals in modern history.

Each homeland was the designated territory of a particular ethnic group, as defined by the government. We were in the former Transkei, which was Xhosa territory. The Xhosa were historically farmers and herders, and they migrated to this part of Africa before the Dutch arrived, making this something of an actual homeland. In 1976, the year before Biko was killed, the Transkei was declared an independent country and its occupants were stripped of their South African citizenship. This allowed the South African government,

was turning to dark, and we walked the rest of the way down an unlit path, led by a young boy who did not speak English. There were no roads in Nqileni, just a handful of dirt tracks. Almost nobody in the village owned a car, and most everyone traveled on foot. The sky was wide and uninterrupted by telephone poles or electrical wires. In the velvety darkness, I could hear waves breaking on the edge of the black expanse that was the Indian Ocean.

Morning revealed a place of extraordinary beauty. The village was located between the Xhora River and the Bulungula River, on rolling hills that overlooked the ocean. The mouth of the Bulungula opened onto long stretches of sand, and mist rose off the shoreline through the mangroves on the bluffs. Low tide exposed rocks crusted with mussel beds, where women carried buckets of mussels on their heads.

The hills above the shore were dotted with smooth round huts, rondavels, painted peach or turquoise or butter yellow. Many were thatched with grass, and others had roofs of corrugated metal. Solar panels were mounted on some, to my surprise. These homes did not have running water or toilets, but they had enough solar energy to charge smartphones.

A woman nicknamed Jabu served as my guide to the village, and frequently as my translator. She was a lively conversationalist who spoke English, which she had learned from tourists in the backpackers' lodge, where women from the village cooked dinners of goat meat and pumpkin leaves for hikers making their way along the Wild Coast. "What is it like for women

the only government that recognized the Transkei, to divest itself of responsibility to the people who lived there. "Separate development" is what this strategy was called—segregation on an enormous scale.

We drove three hundred miles into the former Transkei, past King William's Town (now Qonce), where Steve Biko was born, and through Mvezo, where Nelson Mandela was born. The landscape was a graceful grassland, lightly tattered. There were corrugated metal shacks along the roadsides, and barbed wire fences that had caught bits of trash. Women traveled on paths next to the road, carrying thirty-gallon barrels on their heads. In some places, gashes of erosion had opened in the hillsides, where the land had been overgrazed. Apartheid had starved this region of resources.

The drive took most of a day, the last three hours on unpaved, unmarked roads. When we arrived at a dirt lot on the edge of the village of Nqileni, dusk

in your culture?" Jabu asked as we set off down the path leading from the lodge into the village. I fumbled my answer, getting lost in the minutiae of pay differentials and workplace discrimination. After listening patiently for a few moments, she asked, "Can a woman in your culture choose not to marry?" She knew the answer to this already, as well as the answer to her next question: "If a woman is married, can she have a job?"

Jabu was in her twenties and was the mother of a young child, but had no intention of marrying. Marriage would mean she could not leave the village for work or education. She would be confined to women's work as it was defined there, and she would be expected to wear the traditional dress of a married woman. Three older women sitting in the grass by the side of the path served as her example. Like most people in the village, they spoke only isiXhosa, but they smiled at us and took their role as an exhibit with good humor. They wore scarves knotted over their hair, and long, full skirts, with cloths tied around their waists. Those cloths, Jabu noted, were hot and scratchy.

Jabu wore knit shorts with leggings and ankle boots. Glen had given her a hat emblazoned with the name of the college where he taught, which she tucked over her hair. She would have looked at home in a coffee shop in the college town where I lived, except that she had demonstrated for me the traditional use of river clay as a cosmetic, so her face was covered in white clay. Ghost-faced, in her college-spirit-wear, Jabu knelt on the floor of her mother's rondavel

and ground corn with a large rock, then laughed gently as I struggled to heft the same rock and crush a single kernel.

Women's work in Nqileni involved a considerable amount of heavy lifting. There was the carrying of water, the collecting of firewood, the lugging of buckets of cow dung to resurface the floors, and the excavation of mud to make the bricks from which the rondavels were constructed. This was all the routine maintenance of

life. There was little work in the village that wasn't women's work, but there weren't very many men. When I asked Jabu where the men were, she answered simply, "The mines." Except for the young and the old, most men left the village for work, as they had under apartheid.

"A culture is essentially the society's composite answer to the varied problems of life," Biko wrote in an essay about African theology. The culture Jabu called "my culture" was postapartheid Xhosa culture, which answered problems introduced by apartheid, among other problems. It was a way of life that had been disrupted and undermined, but still maintained. I wanted to blame apartheid for burdening the women of Nqileni, but Jabu understood the source of her outrage to be something far older.

The village headman explained to me, with Jabu as his interpreter, that the crates he used as chairs were reserved for men, and women should sit on the floor. His home was a small rondavel like all the others, mostly empty inside, with a single kerosene burner for cooking, an eroded dirt yard, and a few wandering chickens. The headman was responsible for allocating land and settling disputes in the village. One of my traveling companions asked if people like us, white Americans, would be allowed to move to this village. We could seek permission from the tribal council, the headman responded tactfully, and then added something that made Jabu smirk. If we moved here, we would have to be prepared to open up our private bank accounts, as the members of this village shared everything.

I watched Jabu's face as she listened, alert to every word and every implication. The spotlight of my limited understanding was trained on her, and it was from this position, as Jabu's foreign audience, that I admired her. I didn't know her, but I felt that I recognized her. I saw the little dance move she did to express enthusiastic agreement, and the posture of quiet deference she assumed when translating. I saw the way she expanded her vocabulary, learning and practicing the term

*umbilical cord* over the course of several days. Eventually, she'd like to complete her secondary education, she said, but that would require leaving the village. For now, she had a child to raise, and she wanted to send him to university.

I spent my days in Nqileni walking the paths that rose and fell over the hills. I visited the local radio station where Jabu hosted several radio shows, and I traded polite greetings with one of Jabu's cousins, who wore a red leather jacket with metal studs on the shoulders and red clay on her face. I practiced my four or five words of Xhosa intermittently, with no improvement. After dark, I returned to my rondavel by the lodge, where the dung floor and the thatched roof had filled the room with a grassy scent. I opened a window to the wind coming off the ocean and lay down to read *My Traitor's Heart* with a flashlight. I read without interest then, finding the book suddenly dim and hard to follow. At the far edge of what had once been an unrecognized country, Malan's concerns seemed to belong to another world, the world of white South Africa.

"Mike was my friend, but he didn't trust me," Malan writes. This was his colleague at the paper, a black man who quoted Milton and hummed Handel. They drank together after work, before returning to their segregated neighborhoods, and talked about everything but politics. "If we had talked politics, I would have had to creep and crawl and beg forgiveness for what my people were doing to his. I would have turned into a worm, and Mike into a cripple, a victim." It seems unlikely to me now that Mike would have allowed for that—Mike was a Biko man, a

Black Consciousness man. But I don't doubt that the politics of the moment freighted their friendship.

Malan, who shared a last name with the minister of defense, had been assigned to cover crime in part because he spoke Afrikaans, the language of the police. Working for the newspaper allowed Malan to temporarily defer his military service. When the time came to serve, he left the country. "I ran because I wouldn't carry a gun for apartheid, and because I wouldn't carry a gun against it," he writes. "I ran away because I hated Afrikaners and loved blacks. I ran away because I was an Afrikaner and feared blacks." He fled in a confusion of love and fear. When he returned eight years later, he looked up his old friend Mike. Those years had been hard years in South Africa, years of violent struggle, and Mike was weary. He had been drinking himself to death, he told Malan as they headed to Soweto for a jol, a bender.

At the shebeen where they drank, Mike told anyone who asked that he would vouch for this white man, that he would "go the whole hog for him." This moved Malan, who was always searching Mike for signs of affection. But the night got darker as Mike got drunker. Someone asked if "this whitey was ripe for the picking," and Mike chuckled. Malan asked his drinking companions if this, his whiteness, really needed to come between them. One of them told him that every white man was an enemy, and then affably made an exception for Malan. But Mike was not in the mood to release Malan from his whiteness, and he would not tell him the lie he wanted to hear—that it didn't mean anything.

I felt done with Malan then, after a day of watching people make the most of the starved land that apartheid had left behind. I was tired of Malan's need to be exonerated, and his fixation on being understood as good. I felt far from his desperate desire to be loved by his fellow country people. But that was when I was still in Africa, reading by flashlight. Now, years later, back home under electric lights, I don't feel so far away from Malan's desires. I know what it is to be a tourist in your own country, and I know that's much worse than being a tourist anywhere else.

Jabu marked the conclusion of her tour of women's work by painting the faces of her tourists in the manner that female initiates in the village are painted during the ceremony that marks their transition to adulthood. There was some sly humor to this, as if we Americans had remained children in our insular lives and were awaiting passage into true adulthood even as we entered middle age. But it was an embarrassing spectacle, too, this sacred ritual repurposed as a tourist attraction.

I wanted no part in a fake initiation, but I wanted to be close to Jabu. I wanted to feel the warmth of her breath on my face as she painted my eyelids. In the darkness behind my eyes, that warmth flooded a vast subterranean cavern of teenage loneliness, a loneliness punctuated by an occasional sleepover, a brief encounter with a girl who might give me a tour of her life, dress me in her clothes, and apply makeup to my face, her touch a flicker of intimacy.

Jabu had no reason to trust me, and I knew that, or I would not have hesitated to ask her the question I asked before I left Nqileni. I had avoided this question for as long as I could, until my last day in the village, when we were walking down the path toward the lodge.

"You can write about me," Jabu answered quickly, unconcerned. Then she added, "But I think you should write about Steve Biko." She gave his name the proper isiXhosa pronunciation, "Bee-kaw," so I wasn't sure I understood. "He was killed by the police?" I asked. "Yes," she said. "You should write a poem about Biko. About what they did to him, what they did to people during apartheid."

What the security police did to Biko was detain him for interrogation and then inflict a head injury that caused him to die of brain damage. What the government had already done, years earlier, was declare Biko a banned person. He was confined to the township where he grew up, could not speak in public, could not publish his writing, and could not be quoted in the press.

In the year before his death, Biko was called as a witness in the trial of nine young black men who were accused of treason, not for their actions as much as for their ideas. Black Consciousness itself was on trial. Biko was asked to explain the slogan "Black is beautiful," and several pages of trial transcript were dedicated to an interrogation of the word *black*, during which the judge asked, "But now why do you refer to you people as blacks? Why not brown people?"

Biko used the term *black* expansively, not just for indigenous Africans. *Black* was an inversion of *non-white*, the collective term used by the government for an ever-increasing array of racial categories, including Colored, Bantu, Indian, and Malay. These categories were, Biko recognized, a divisive strategy. *Black* was a gesture of solidarity, whereas *non-white* was a term of exclusion. To be called *non-white* was to be defined in the negative, Biko argued, defined by what you weren't. To choose *black* was to define yourself in the positive.

Under apartheid logic, being pro-black could only mean being anti-white. This is what Donald Woods, a white newspaper editor, feared when he first met Biko. Woods was opposed to apartheid, but he was also opposed to Black Consciousness. He misunderstood it as a claim to cultural superiority. Black pride, he thought, was as racist as Afrikaner nationalism. And he resented being reduced to his race. "I don't have to bloody well apologize for being born white or for racial policies I don't support!" Woods told Biko during their first meeting. At this, Biko grinned and settled back into his chair.

Biko wasn't asking for any apologies, and he wasn't interested in reproducing apartheid with black tyrants in place of white tyrants. He wanted more than "a mere change of face" in the government—he wanted an entirely new system of governance. Biko had nothing against white liberals as individuals, he explained, but he didn't believe that black liberation could be achieved under white leadership. White liberals were too comfortable, and their goals were too limited. He wouldn't compromise on his most basic rights, and whatever hurt feelings this caused couldn't be his concern.

By the end of that first meeting, Woods had agreed to hire a black reporter to write a column on Black Consciousness. As Biko walked Woods to his car, he pretended to shield his eyes from the blinding glow of the Mercedes, one of the spoils of apartheid. They became friends, and Biko never stopped ribbing Woods about the Mercedes, which, Woods protested, was the "smallest, cheapest" Mercedes available.

Early in their friendship, Woods tried to impress Biko by offering to bring him to a restaurant where black people could not ordinarily dine with white people. Biko was not impressed, they did not go to the restaurant, and that, Woods noted, was his last act of

"token integration," though it was not his last blunder. Both men had political ambitions and loved nothing more than long conversations about political strategy, so this was not an unlikely friendship. But it was opposed by every force in the country, including the police force.

To evade the security police, Woods and Biko sometimes used puns on isiXhosa words as a code when they arranged their meetings. Woods had grown up in the Transkei, where he'd learned to speak isiXhosa from his playmates. Those Xhosa children didn't have schools, so they couldn't read, and it had never occurred to Woods that his black playmates were his intellectual equals—not until he met Biko. Opposed

to apartheid as he was, apartheid had nonetheless left a mark on his mind.

After Biko's death, Woods was declared a banned person for his association with Biko. He could not write for the newspaper or appear in public, he was surveilled and harassed, his family was threatened, and he eventually fled South Africa to publish his book *Biko*, which includes long passages of Biko's own words, smuggled out of a country that refused to print them. The book, like *My Traitor's Heart*, is an indictment of white liberalism, written by a white liberal.

Biko himself, writing under the name Frank Talk, had a few things to say about white liberals. They believed fervently in the "myth of integration" and were eager to promote integration alone as the solution to a problem that would, in the end, long outlast apartheid. This problem was the concentration of wealth and property in the hands of a white minority. The psychic shadow cast by the concept of racial superiority would also outlast apartheid. White liberals were preoccupied with maintaining their moral superiority, Biko wrote, and wasted too much energy proving their liberalness to one another and performing it for black people. "If they are true liberals," he insisted, "they must realize that they themselves are oppressed."

Biko was killed the year I was born, 1977, but none of what he writes about white liberals seems of the past to me, or of another place. Nor does the manner of his death: beaten by the police. Here in the suburbs of Chicago, the integration of the public schools is still commonly regarded as the solution to a much bigger problem. We are housed within this problem, in properties whose value has been artificially inflated or deflated by redlining and zoning laws. Not long ago, this historically progressive town had separate hospitals for white people and black people, and separate YMCAs. The aftermath of apartheid is still unfolding here, and the past is still playing out. One needs only to read the local papers, or listen in on conversations within the PTA, to witness amateur actors delivering poorly performed versions of Biko's first conversation with Donald Woods. I myself have rehearsed that conversation several times, sometimes playing Woods, and sometimes playing Biko.

Like Woods, I feel hurt when I'm not seen for who I am, and like Biko, I'm aware of more pressing concerns. The United States incarcerates more of its own people than South Africa did at the height of apartheid. I know this, but I don't feel it every day, in part because I'm protected from it. What I feel every day are the stresses in my relationships with friends and colleagues and neighbors. The assumptions, the misunderstandings, the discomfort that is spoken and unspoken. The reality that we are not equals before the law.

Unspooling alongside every interaction is a filmstrip of who we are, a supercut of unsteady footage. In one video, shot in a New Jersey mall, a fistfight begins between two teenagers when a light-skinned boy pushes a black boy. Police break up the fight and sit the light-skinned boy down on a couch while both officers kneel on the back of the black boy and

handcuff him. The light-skinned boy, who will later clarify that he is not white and call the arrest of the other boy "plain old racist," watches from the couch. This viral video was texted to me by the father of one of my son's friends. An explanation followed, but I knew what he wanted me to see.

*Friends Disappear* is the title of a book about this town where we live. The author, Mary Barr, begins with a photo of her childhood friends sitting on the front steps of a house. They have all just graduated from eighth grade at the middle school where my son is now in eighth grade. The date of the photo is 1974, when the school district had been desegregated for five years. Six of the teenagers are black and seven are white. They are sitting shoulder to shoulder, two with their arms linked, one on another's lap. They are close. But the white kids and the black kids won't remain friends in high school. They will hardly see one another. By the time Barr tracks down every person in the photo, thirty years later, two of the black boys will be dead—one killed in a confrontation with the police, another in a crash during a police chase.

All but one of the teenagers in the photo "flirted with delinquency," according to Barr. They smoked pot, they drank, they skipped classes, they got bad grades. Two of the white kids dropped out and finished their degrees at night school, but all the white kids went on to prosperous futures. Only one of their black friends made it to the middle class.

There is a persistently naive belief, common among white liberals, that fostering friendships between children of different racial backgrounds will heal the division cleaved into this country by American apartheid. Friendship, in other words, is seen as the solution to a problem that threatens lasting friendship.

I once sat in a restorative-justice circle at my local elementary school, where a white parent new to the district told the circle that he wanted his children to have black friends. Asked if he had any black friends, he admitted in dismay, "No, not here." Within that circle, this was understood as a personal failure, rather than a consequence of the long aftermath of apartheid.

Love and friendship are undermined by the same policies that undermine education and homeownership. Redlining devalued black property and left American cities gutted—so, too, with interracial relationships. We have railroads running between us, highways, sanitary canals. This is part of the everyday agony of living in a postapartheid state. Is this agony the worst of it? Not by far. But it is agony, nonetheless.

"The American landscape was once graced with resplendent public swimming pools, some big enough to hold thousands of swimmers at a time," Heather McGhee writes in her book *The Sum of Us*. In the 1950s, under pressure to integrate those pools, some towns transformed them into members-only private swim clubs. Others drained their pools and let them sit empty. In St. Louis, the first integrated swim at the largest public pool in the country ended with a white mob attacking the black swimmers. In Montgomery, Alabama, the grand Oak Park pool was filled with dirt and paved over. I now think of the gaps in my life, in my relationships—the silences, the losses, the failures, the distances—as swimming pools filled with dirt.

Shortly before I left for South Africa, a friend told me that her wife, a banker, worked with a white man from South Africa who had once said, "It's hard to be a white man in South Africa." That phrase became a joke between my friend and her wife, something one of them would say if she happened to catch the other looking out of touch or self-involved: upset that the lawn service had failed to eradicate the dandelions, for instance. I found this joke funny even as I believed something of the earnest sentiment. Not that it is hard to be a white man in South Africa, but that it is hard to reclaim your own mind from apartheid.

"It was harder than ever to be white and conscious," Malan writes of the final years before the end of apartheid—meaning that many of the white people in his circle didn't know what to do with their consciousness. Understanding their position in what Biko called "the system" made them want to escape that position, but they saw no way out. A "people without a positive history is like a vehicle without an engine," as Biko put it, referring to an apartheid education that taught African history as a series of deficiencies and defeats. Malan, who recognized the history of his people in Africa as a history of hatred given and received, found himself without an engine. He hated Afrikaners for being bigots, and he hated liberal whites for being ineffectual. He had no tribe.

White people are, as a group, hard to love. We can also be difficult as individuals. When we look at one another, we don't always like what we see. There's a white South African woman in my town who runs a website that informs white residents about issues of relevance to black residents. I haven't met her, but I've seen her interviewed in a film, and even before she said anything, I was distancing myself from her in my mind. She had lived here for almost twenty years, she said, and she'd once thought she lived in a diverse community. But at some point she noticed that all her friends were white, and that she knew nothing about the black community or its history. As a child growing up under apartheid, she said, she felt guilty, and uncomfortable, and helpless. There, at the word *helpless*, the distance closed. I, too, felt helpless, and I hated to admit it.

"I have told you several murder stories, but the true subject of this narrative has been the divided state of my own heart," Malan confesses in his final chapter, the chapter he rewrote for the paperback published a year after the first edition. Mandela had been released from prison by then, and Malan was still revising a book that had already gone to print. Both endings read as an unsolved problem. The closest Malan comes to putting this problem into words is "I was searching for a way to live in this strange country."

I spent my last hours in South Africa walking the wide, pleasant paths of Green Point Park in Cape Town. The previous day, we had driven

past miles and miles of tightly packed metal shacks flanked by rows of concrete outhouses near the edge of the highway, through the bleakest landscape I had ever seen, to a school in Makhaza township where children danced for us. At the end of the performance, Glen got up and danced the jive while I quietly wept, hiding my tears. Those tears were the product of the education I'd come for. And so, educated, I walked through the park

in a rage. To hell with this country, I was thinking. A white woman came along the path with a child on a tricycle, trailing glittering red steamers from the handles, spangled by sunlight. I looked through the woman's smile into her skull, and thought, How do you live with yourself? The answer to this question came to me instantaneously. She lives with herself, my mind told me, in exactly the same way you do. ✳

... A HISTORY THAT HEARKENS BACK TO SCIENCE FICTION PUBLICATIONS.

FAN LETTERS WOULD BE PRINTED IN LETTER COLUMNS, AND BECAUSE FULL ADDRESSES WERE PRINTED BACK THEN, FANS COULD WRITE TO ONE ANOTHER — AS FAR BACK AS THE 1930s!

AND SOME LETTER WRITERS WOULD LATER BECOME PROMINENT PROFESSIONALS. IN THE COMICS WORLD, THESE INCLUDED...

KURT BUSIEK

PAUL LEVITZ

ROY THOMAS

MY TITANS LETTER ASKED ABOUT **TITAN TALK**, A FANZINE.

IT WAS A PLEA FOR SOMETHING I DESPERATELY WANTED: ANYONE IN THE WORLD TO TALK WITH ABOUT COMICS.

EDITOR'S NOTE: THIS WAS BEFORE THE INTERNET, KIDS!!

MY LETTER ALSO ASKED FOR PEN PALS.

THAT WOULD UNEXPECTEDLY HELP WITH SOMETHING *ELSE* I WAS SILENT ABOUT...

... BEING GAY.

ONE OF MY NEW PEN PALS WAS A FELLOW *LEGION OF SUPER-HEROES* SUPERFAN.

AFTER A FEW EXCHANGES, WE TOLD EACH OTHER WE WERE GAY.

HIS LETTERS WERE THEN WRITTEN IN *INTERLAC*, THE UNIVERSAL LANGUAGE OF THE LEGION AND ITS 31ST-CENTURY WORLD.

HE COULD TELL ME ABOUT HIS EXPERIENCES, WITH NO FEAR THAT HIS PARENTS (OR MINE!) COULD READ THEM.

I WAS AS IMPRESSED THAT HE OWNED A COMPUTER AS I WAS THAT HE HAD AN INTERLAC CUSTOM FONT!

I SOON MET ANOTHER GAY LEGION PEN PAL IN PERSON. WE MET FOR A DRINK IN MIDTOWN MANHATTAN.

I WAS AROUND 19; JIM WAS AROUND 31.

I REMEMBER HIS VIBRANT BLUE EYES AND THE HIGH-VOLTAGE *JOLT* OF FINDING SOMEONE WHOM I COULD ASPIRE TO BE:

AN ADULT GAY MAN, WITH A PROFESSION AND A PARTNER, WHO WAS **OUT**.

JIM HAD RECENTLY MET KEVIN — AND THEY ARE STILL TOGETHER.

(We reconnected in 2015 and Jim helped fact-check this.)

I WROTE IN ABOUT POWER GIRL #1, A MINI-SERIES IN 1988. THE LETTER TELEGRAPHED HOW IMMATURE, AND GAY, I AM:

I HAD MODEST SUCCESS GETTING PRINTED — BECAUSE I WAS FAST.

" She's
hot.
She's
sexy.
She's
stacked. "

( WHAT WAS I THINKING?! )

I WOULD READ MY WEEKLY STACK, PLUG IN THE TYPEWRITER, AND MAIL MY LETTERS WITHIN A DAY.

AND THIS WAS BEFORE POWER GIRL'S INCREASINGLY AMPLE CHEST WARRANTED A DOUBLE-PAGE SPREAD IN DC'S WHO'S WHO.

I EVEN COMMENTED ON MINI-SERIES, WHICH DID NOT ALWAYS CARRY LETTER COLUMNS.

I'M MUCH MORE PROUD OF A 1989 LETTER IN HAWK AND DOVE, ANOTHER MINI. IN 2018, THE WRITER GEOFF JOHNS, WHO HAD RESCUED ONE-HALF OF THIS DUO FROM OBSCURITY, POSTED MY LETTER ON FACEBOOK. I STAND BY IT:

WRITING LETTERS WAS FREEING.

MY 1995 MISSIVE IN LEGIONNAIRES #23 NOTED:

" The new team is exciting and cuter than ever. (Ah, Cosmic Boy.) "

" I love the new Dove. She looks stunning and has great moves.

Hawk does not deserve her. "

( DESPITE BEING BARELY OUT OF THE CLOSET IN REAL LIFE. )

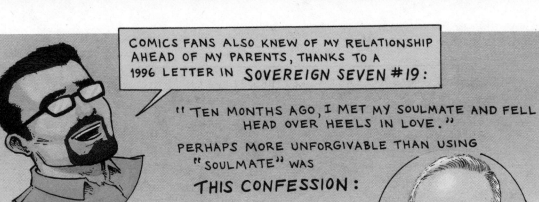

COMICS FANS ALSO KNEW OF MY RELATIONSHIP AHEAD OF MY PARENTS, THANKS TO A 1996 LETTER IN **SOVEREIGN SEVEN #19**:

"TEN MONTHS AGO, I MET MY SOULMATE AND FELL HEAD OVER HEELS IN LOVE."

PERHAPS MORE UNFORGIVABLE THAN USING "SOULMATE" WAS

**THIS CONFESSION:**

STEVE

"MY INTEREST IN COMICS HAD BEEN DWINDLING AT THE TIME."

( COMICS LURED ME BACK, OF COURSE — AND MY "SOULMATE" AND I ARE NOW MARRIED. )

By 1997, I WAS PRACTICALLY A GAY ACTIVIST!

IN **YOUNG HEROES IN LOVE #5**, I MUSED:

"DARE I HOPE WE'LL SEE THE APPEARANCE OF A GAY SUPER-HERO? I MEAN, GAY SUPER-HEROES FALL IN LOVE TOO, RIGHT? YOU COULD EVEN NAME THE HERO AFTER ME."

COINCIDENTALLY, THAT WISH CAME TRUE IN THE SAME YEAR —

"THERMAL UNIT" FROM **CRIMSON PLAGUE #1** IS NAMED...

code name: THERMAL UNIT

birth name: GEORGE GUSTINES

( THANK YOU, GEORGE PÉREZ! )

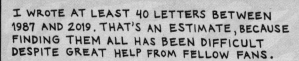

I WROTE AT LEAST 40 LETTERS BETWEEN 1987 AND 2019. THAT'S AN ESTIMATE, BECAUSE FINDING THEM ALL HAS BEEN DIFFICULT DESPITE GREAT HELP FROM FELLOW FANS.

ONE FAN POINTED ME TO COMICS.ORG...

...A SITE WHOSE SEARCHABLE DATABASE OF CREDITS INCLUDES – THE LETTERHACKS!

THIS ONLINE RESOURCE CITES NAMES OF THOSE WHO WERE PUBLISHED IN LETTER COLUMNS.

EVEN SO, A COMICS GEEK ON SOCIAL MEDIA FOUND A LETTER IN *THE SPECTRE #19* NOT LISTED THERE.

ONLINE PLEAS TO LOCATE ALL MY LETTERS WERE SPEEDILY MET WITH SCANS AND PHOTOS.

IN 2017, TONY, THE ARTIST OF THIS STORY, GAVE ME A COPY OF JLA #18 WITH ONE OF MY LETTERS.

MY MOST RECENT LETTER WAS IN CAPTAIN MARVEL #1 (2019).

I LOVED THE ISSUE AND WAS ALSO MOTIVATED TO ADD IT TO A COLLAGE LAYOUT OF COMICS COVERS WITH MY LETTERS.

My OCD is ridiculous.

ONE OF MY REPORTING EXPERIENCES WAS COVERING LOOT, A BROOKLYN STORE THAT FOCUSES ON TEACHING KIDS ABOUT COMICS.

I SPOTTED BATMAN #422 ON THE WALLS, WHILE INTERVIEWING THE OWNER.

YUP, IT CONTAINS ONE OF MY LETTERS.

WE BOTH GOT A KICK OUT OF IT.

IN 2019, MY BUDDY ALLIE GAVE ME SEVEN SEEMINGLY RANDOM COMICS FOR MY BIRTHDAY.

I'M CLEARLY NOT THE WORLD'S GREATEST DETECTIVE, BECAUSE IT TOOK ME A FEW MINUTES TO REALIZE THEY EACH HAD ONE OF MY LETTERS!

I tease myself a lot about the quality of these letters — though a recent search turned up a few more, one of which struck me as a solid letter about the Justice Society ...

... but I'm proud of them. They solidified my fandom, helped me form long-lasting connections, and gave me the confidence to pursue an unexpected career path —

— writing about comics for The New York Times.

Bruce&
Clark&
Diana&
Hal&
Arthur&
Barry&
J'onn.

LONG LIVE COMICS!
GEORGE & TONY & MEESEY.

# THE RADIANT FORCE OF THE INCLINE

In praise of the briefly famous Caribbean author Eric Walrond and other writers who skirt great expectations

by **MEARA SHARMA**

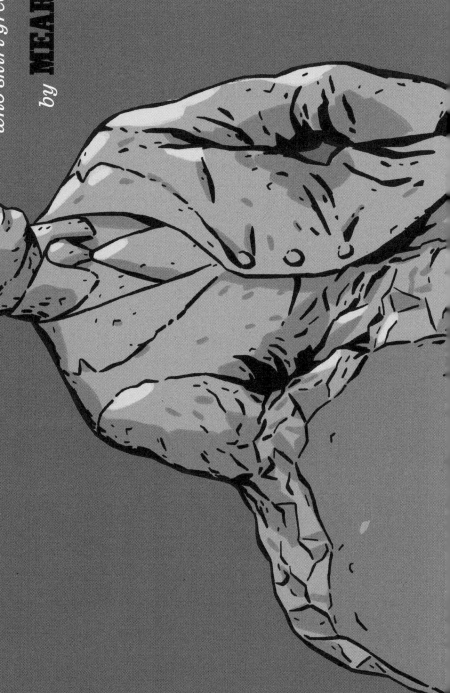

ILLUSTRATIONS THROUGHOUT BY:
*Kristian Hammerstad*

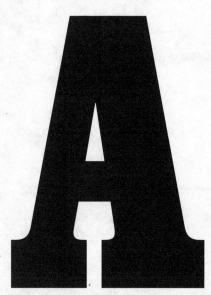

**A**bout five winters ago, I spent a lot of time wandering around London's cemeteries. Not so much the famously occupied ones, with their hulking tombs and majestic statues, like Highgate, where Karl Marx and George Michael share soil, or Westminster Abbey, a real who's who of Western achievement, housing everyone from Isaac Newton to Charles Dickens to Stephen Hawking. No, I preferred the ordinary, scraggly cemeteries, tucked into the outer boroughs, where crooked, ivy-choked gravestones teeter atop earth that buckles and splits from the creeping roots of trees, and people have names like Elswyth Wivelsfield.

I had recently left New York City, where I'd had a steady day job in journalism, a steady side hustle with a literary magazine, a steady relationship, and a steady social network. When I moved to London, I had none of those things—by choice. After years in a cocoon of stability, it was thrilling to shed it all, to expose myself to the elements. Colors shone brighter, rain felt fresher. Any sense of a predetermined future fell away, and in that empty space was possibility. I was ecstatically free. But I was also painfully lonely, sharing a basement apartment with a moody seventy-three-year-old theater director and struggling to meet people and find work in an unfamiliar city. My neighborhood was gushing with attractive, artsy young souls who all looked like they could be my friends, but they weren't. I was floating. Cemeteries were, quite literally, grounding.

I suppose, in the absence of living pals, it was nice to be among past lives. There was no pressure to introduce myself. All encounters were speculative, subject only to my own whims. And in a moment when I was meant to be figuring out what to do with my life, when the paradox of choice was often crippling, there was something reassuring about a cemetery's capacity to distill a life to its basics. All you really need to know is right there. Here lies Heremod Shipley, cherished father of Holly and James, beloved husband of Philomena. Lovella Moresbeth: She truly *loved* her family. Lives rendered in brief, appropriately and pleasingly mundane. It can be simple, in the end.

So there I was, one winter afternoon, in North London's Abney Park cemetery, doing my thing. Erasmus Septimus Eyre sounded like he got up to something shady in the colonies. Isabella Titmarsh fell asleep at age thirteen; I wonder what happened? Edwina Thimbleby drowned while rescuing her sister! But overall, everyone was a good parent, a treasured sibling, an upstanding neighbor—with a cozy English name to boot. I was comforted by the platitudes, the predictability, the homeliness of it all, the refreshing absence of angst and uncertainty and regret. Until I came across a gravestone with a different sort of declaration.

ERIC D. WALROND
AUTHOR OF
TROPIC DEATH
1898–1966

At the top of the stone there was a semiabstract carving of a figure standing behind an oversize book and quill. And then, in stocky block letters, the sparse epitaph. No reference to a doting spouse, a brood of children, a military legacy. Just… the author of a single titillatingly titled book. It struck me as confident as well as tragic; brazen, yet somehow defensive; amusing, but also haunting. Who was this man, this writer, who wanted to be remembered like this, free of family or place or God's love, but for one and only one work? The emphasis implied an absence, an obfuscation. A story.

As I stood before the grave, a quick google revealed some basic facts. Eric Derwent Walrond passed his childhood in British colonial–era Guiana and Barbados and canal-era Panama, before moving to New York City in 1918, at the age of nineteen. There he got a job with Marcus Garvey's newspaper and became friends with writers and artists who would go on to define the Harlem Renaissance, including Langston Hughes, Countee Cullen, and Zora Neale Hurston. At age twenty-eight, in 1926, he published a short-story collection titled *Tropic Death*, among the first works of American fiction to unspool Caribbean lives. The book was fervently praised by major critics and thinkers, including W.E.B. Du Bois. Walrond was anointed a rising star, a key figure in the New Negro literary movement, and was given another book deal. The next year, he won a Guggenheim Fellowship.

Then the details start to dwindle. Walrond left New York just as fame and fortune beckoned. He traveled around the Caribbean and lived briefly in Paris. Then in London. Then in the rural southwest of England. Years elapsed. His writing output became sporadic: a story here, an essay there, a bit of this, a bit of that. He fell out of touch with his New York friends and fellow luminaries. He took on work as an accountant, and in factories. He spent some time as a patient at a mental hospital. He died of a heart attack in 1966, at the age of sixty-seven, alone on a London street. He never published another book.

It's a bleak narrative. Exceptionally promising young person from immigrant background loses his way and fails to live up to expectations, while his friends become household names. I thought of the many brilliant people I know who are struggling to find their place. I thought of talented friends whose stars were rising—would it last? I thought of myself, my own French exit from literary New York City in my late twenties. I, too, left the promised land right when opportunities to further my career seemed to be opening up, right when my contemporaries were beginning to make inroads. I, too, chose to relocate, somewhat inexplicably, to the nation that had colonized my ancestors (for I, too, originate from a place once ruled by the British: India). Was moving to London a huge mistake? Am I squandering my potential? Will I die alone here, on a smog-choked street? Get me back to the dutiful Christians and the stalwart spouses, the lives that shut cleanly like a box. I sped along to more reassuring terrain. Here lie the bodies of Herbert and Henrietta Hudson, finally together again, too well loved ever to be forgotten. Existential crisis averted, order restored.

Before long, this brief encounter with Walrond faded from view. And years elapsed. Eventually I made living friends in London and therefore stopped walking in cemeteries. I toyed with unfamiliar worlds and communities, enjoying the peripheral vantage point of an expat (a word that, I like to think, derives not just from the Latin *expatriatus*, meaning "gone out from one's country," but also from *exspatiari*, meaning "to move beyond one's usual bounds"). While forging a new life, I lost touch, inevitably, with many people from my old one. But reinvention afforded me a sense of artistic freedom I hadn't felt in the United States, and I began to focus on

writing creatively, something I had long wanted to devote myself to. My output was sporadic—a story here, an essay there, a bit of this, a bit of that—and I was unsure where it might lead, but I was content, happy in the searching.

And then, in 2023, as I was preparing to uproot again, this time for Scotland, I found myself back in a cemetery. Perhaps, in the face of imminent change, I was drawn, unconsciously, to well-trodden ground. Wandering the muddy paths, thinking of arrivals and departures, losses and gains, decisions to leave, decisions to stay, I suddenly remembered the young man from the Caribbean who, for a time, was destined for greatness. The arc of his story—not quite a rise and fall, but a rise and fizzle. How he kept leaving: leaving the Caribbean, leaving New York, leaving Paris, leaving London. What his friends, like some of mine, might have said: *Here you go again, jettisoning a world you've built, choosing uncertainty over continuity, choosing to disperse rather than concentrate, to scatter rather than root. At what cost?* In the shadow of my own departure, the silhouette of Eric Walrond's story pressed up from the depths, and this time it firmly took hold. This peripatetic, largely forgotten writer started to become not merely a cautionary tale but a kind of mirror image, a screen and a surrogate for my own questions about artistic success, and failure, and the gray area in between.

The specter of failure, of course, looms large over creative people, whose identities are particularly bound up with their work; the stock character of the tortured artist dates back to Plato. Culturally, we tend to romanticize grandiose failure—artists who toiled in bitter agony or isolation or with complete lack of recognition their whole lives, only to become demigods after death (van Gogh, Emily Dickinson). In an essay in *Boston Review*, the critic Tom Bissell considers how fragile the phenomenon of writerly success is, exploring how names that are iconic and enduring today, like Herman Melville and Walt Whitman, could easily have been long lost, had it not been for an assortment of arbitrary occurrences: "Remaindered copies bought from book peddlers. A man, sitting at his desk, an oxidized copy of a forgotten novel beside him, cobbling together an essay with no idea of what it would accomplish.… Essays published at the right time, in the right journals or books, noticed by the right people." The reasons many famous writers of yore continue to have star status has little to do with fate, Bissell writes, but rather with "the stagecraft of chance." He quotes Melville—notoriously unsuccessful in his lifetime, writing to a friend in 1849 upon the flop of his novel *Mardi*. "[It] may possibly—by some miracle, that is—flower like aloe, a hundred years hence—or not flower at all, which is more likely by far, for some aloes never flower."

A lifetime of failure and then posthumous success is one thing. It's a more movie-friendly narrative arc. But what do we do with the stories of people, like Walrond, who were poised to take off but never fully did? Who didn't lose the game but didn't quite win, either, in life or in death? Whose aloes might have flowered a little too soon, and then—slowly, unceremoniously—withered on the vine?

I soon discover that since Eric Walrond's death, in 1966, there have in fact been a couple of attempts to resuscitate his story and reappraise his work in the context of his era and contemporaries. The first is a 2013 reissue of *Tropic Death* from Walrond's own publisher, Liveright (then Boni & Liveright). The edition declares the short-story collection a "lost classic of the Harlem Renaissance," one that was endorsed by Langston Hughes for its "hard poetic beauty." Deeply informed by Walrond's upbringing in Guiana, Barbados, and Panama in the early twentieth century, the book is a stunning immersion in the struggles of poor Black and brown people in the Caribbean, whose lives are marked by disease and death, oppressive foreign influence, and the tyrannical force of the sun, which blazes on almost every page ("O tireless, sleepless sun! It burned and kissed things"), as well as a throbbing determination. As Arnold Rampersad writes in his introduction, "Life is both effulgent, in that it reflects tropical richness, and also stringent, pinching." Walrond's language is sensuous, hallucinatory, dense with modernist innovations as well as dialect-rich regional voices. As in "Drought," when a father overhears a doctor inspecting his dead child:

It came to Coggins in swirls. Autopsy. Noise comes in swirls. Pounding, pounding—dry Indian corn pounding. Ginger. Ginger being pounded in a mortar with a bright, new pestle. Pound, pound. And. Sawing. Butcher shop. Cow foot is sawed that way. Stew—or tough hard steak. Then the drilling—drilling—drilling to a stone cutter's ears. Ox grizzle. Drilling into ox grizzle…

"Too bad, Coggins," the doctor said, "too bad, to lose yo' dawtah…"

With its commitment to local modes of speech, the book belongs, Rampersad argues, "with a number of key books by authors who practically revolutionized the idea of regionalism in America and elsewhere," namely *Adventures of Huckleberry Finn*, *Dubliners*, and *The Sound and the Fury*. But Walrond's "life of vagabondage and exile" has long left *Tropic Death* underappreciated.

The other significant effort to revive Walrond comes in the form of a 2015 biography by James Davis, professor of American studies and English at Brooklyn College. *Eric Walrond: A Life in the Harlem Renaissance and the Transatlantic Caribbean*, published by Columbia University Press, is an ambitious and sensitive attempt to trace Walrond's itinerant existence, critically assess the scope of his work as a Caribbean diasporic writer, and flesh out the struggles and motivations that shaped him. Through correspondence, mentions in essays, newspaper articles, and other scattered appearances, Davis pieces together the twists and turns of Walrond's life and his abiding dedication to writing—an impressive feat, given that a cohesive stash of Walrond's papers doesn't exist. Davis quotes Saidiya Hartman: "The archive dictates what can be said about the past," and his book is a moving attempt to write Walrond firmly into the archive and, indeed, recast the tale of his life as one characterized by ongoing courage and perseverance rather than simply unfulfilled expectations.

Walrond was descended from an African slave and a Scottish planter, and as such, from childhood his life was defined by movement between places and worlds, disorientation, paradoxes, and code-switching. When he was a young boy in British colonial Guiana, his family strove for middle-class respectability (his father was a tailor) amid labor unrest on sugar plantations. Then, in Barbados, his starched collars and genteel British education—Latin and Greek, a schoolyard laced with Union Jacks—contrasted with the impoverished, drought-plagued neighborhood in which he lived. As Davis writes, Barbados deeply informed Walrond's later writing, becoming "his muse, color palette, and mental grammar, cultivating an exuberant and promiscuous lexicon, a knowledge of formal and folk speech, and a Victorian sensibility toward public and professional life."

When he was in his early teens, he and his family migrated again, to the swampy, pulsating Canal Zone of Colón, Panama, a transnational mash-up of West Indian, Asian, Spanish, North American, and Indigenous people. Walrond lived in a West Indian slum with his family, and the pestilent underbelly of the city became his playground. He also confronted the American import of Jim Crow segregation and the flattening racial category of "Negro," which, naturally, politicized him. But despite being denied access to an education on par with that of white children, he was able to continue his schooling through private tutors, and his linguistic abilities and sheer determination ultimately landed him a job at the *Star & Herald*, a major Latin American daily. When he was eighteen, his beat consisted of "brawls, murders, political scandals, voodoo rituals, labor confabs, campaigns, concerts, dramatic affairs, shipping intelligence…" Before long, the ambitious young writer "got to the point where I thought I must be moving out into a bigger world of endeavor. So before I knew it *I was on my way to America!*"

He arrived on Ellis Island in June 1918, at age nineteen and a half, and moved in with his aunt in the Caribbean enclave of Bedford-Stuyvesant, Brooklyn—a place that felt at once familiar and strange, like home and also foreign—before packing up and moving to Harlem. While negotiating a series of odd jobs, from porter to dish slinger to longshoreman, Walrond wrote a few essays inveighing against colonialism and racism. Then a speculative short story about a successful back-to-Africa movement he'd penned for a contest attracted the attention of Marcus Garvey and landed him a job at Garvey's newspaper, *Negro World*.

From there Walrond's star quickly, astonishingly rose, as he wrote his way beyond Black periodicals and into the mainstream. "Within four years," Davis writes, "he would be dining downtown with Alfred and Blanche Knopf, James Weldon Johnson, Carl Van Vechten, Zora Neale Hurston, Countee Cullen, Langston Hughes, Alain Locke, and other literati. He would take them to A'Lelia Walker's parties, heir to the fortune of the first African American millionaire, and dance the Charleston until the early morning in the gin-soaked cabarets of

Prohibition-era Harlem. It was a vertiginous ascent from which he would not soon recover." Thanks to the support of a patron, Walrond received free lodging and a stipend, allowing him to work on the fiction that would go on to become *Tropic Death*. He was constantly being called "promising" and "brilliant," and seemed adept at harnessing his enviable combination of intellect, ambition, and charisma—but his private letters, as Davis unearths, also reveal struggles with depression. "This high-strung, unnatural, morbid, discontented state of mind," he wrote to a friend. "I am such a furiously emotional creature.… in this raw, briny, floundering state."

After winning a fiction prize in 1925, he wrote to another friend: "I am particularly depressed these days, that is why I didn't write you before, and I am actually engaged in the absorbing process of counting the minutes of my existence—as if I were a condemned man." Nonetheless, a year later, *Tropic Death* was published to great fanfare, with glowing reviews in *The New Yorker*, *The New Republic*, *The New York Times*, and beyond. Donald Friede, vice president of Boni & Liveright, ordained Walrond "the outstanding Negro prose writer of this country… I believe that his work will in time place him among the important writers in America—both

Negro and white." Scholarships, prizes, a Guggenheim Fellowship, and a whirlwind of other opportunities flowed from there.

A more foreboding version of this appraisal of Walrond is echoed in Wallace Thurman's 1930 essay "This Negro Literary Renaissance": "None is more ambitious than he, none more possessed of keener observation, poetic insight or intelligence.… His prose demonstrates his struggles to escape from conventionalities and become an individual talent. But so far this struggle has not been crowned with any appreciable success.… Will he or will he not cross the Rubicon? It is to be hoped that he will, for he is truly too talented, too sincere an individual and artist to die aborning." In fact, Davis points out that at the height of his fame, Walrond crossed a different sort of Rubicon, leaving the United States for Europe: Paris and the South of France, and then the United Kingdom. Why? On the one hand, his movements were in keeping with the patterns of his contemporaries, and with a sort of diasporic circuit; Countee Cullen and Langston Hughes also spent time in Paris. But he seemed to be in search of a mental respite from the yoke of expectation, and a fresh start after negotiations with his publisher about a second book—a history of Panama—humiliatingly fell apart.

On to London, which in the early 1930s was experiencing an influx of writers from the colonies, many of whom Walrond came to know. He wrote on race relations and the paradoxes of colonialism, Englishness, Caribbeanness, and the formation of Black British identity. But by and large, he struggled to find a place for himself in this new

milieu, with its own set of politics and idiosyncrasies, and in turn struggled to place his work. A generation later, writers of Caribbean descent would articulate their experiences in the mainstream, but perhaps Walrond was too ahead of his time. Why did he stay in England, then, if it wasn't quite working out? There were rumors of Walrond planning to return to New York, though he didn't. Perhaps, as a former colonial subject himself, he felt a complex draw to Britain and a strange sense of belonging there. This is a feeling I have often had, and struggled to articulate, as a person of Indian origin: that postcolonial Britain is somehow more home than America. For the connection between the colonizer and the colonized—however fraught, violent, unjust—runs deep.

Whatever the explanation, he remained in the city, all the while growing increasingly reclusive, and becoming "very successful at dodging people he didn't want to know or that he didn't want to talk with." He was embarrassed, it seems, by his floundering, by his sense of having disappointed people. So inevitably, he fell off the map. Back in Harlem, the refrain *What happened to Eric Walrond?* began to resound.

A few years later, as World War II broke out, Walrond evacuated London for rural Bradford-on-Avon, where he remained, for the next thirteen years, the only Black man in a town of four thousand. From his small stone cottage, he wrote war reports and the occasional review for an assortment of Black periodicals, worked at a rubber factory to make ends meet, and became ever more isolated and depressed. Very few people in town seemed to know he was a writer, let alone a nearly famous one. It must have been painful to watch from afar as friends from his past life became increasingly public figures. I imagine the feeling might have also been tinged with a kind of bittersweet pride—*I was there, at the beginning; it could just as well have been me.*

In 1952, at age fifty-four, he admitted himself to the Roundway mental hospital. The place was vast and under-resourced, but the staff were progressive and kind, and helped Walrond find a sense of stability, purpose, and companionship he had long lacked. He even excitedly threw himself into starting a literary magazine, *The Roundway Review*. Though it was a long way from his glittering days among the New York literati, I was heartened by this turn in Walrond's tale. The magazine seemed to give him real pleasure; he was its most active contributor, as Davis points out, appearing in forty of the first fifty issues. In this humble journal, he published fiction set in his many homes, from Guiana and Barbados to the USA and England. He serialized a deeply researched history of the French canal attempt in Panama over fifteen issues—the only surviving element of his long-floundering manuscript "The Big Ditch." "There is something at once wonderful and tragic," Davis writes, "about the juxtaposition in these pages of some of the earliest Caribbean stories published in England and a startling work of colonial history, alongside other patients' tributes to the hospital band and reminiscences about a favorite horse at a nearby farm."

In 1957, Walrond's stint at Roundway came to an end when he received an opportunity, via one of his old New York contacts, to curate a theatrical program of Black poets in London. He was delighted to be asked, and, after eighteen years away, was quick to pack up and move back to London for the gig, even though the work itself was meagerly paid. He saw the project as a vital and thrilling opportunity to showcase the great achievements of Black artists at a time of increasingly strained race relations. Also, the assignment gave him hope that he had not been entirely forgotten.

While staying in a student hotel and struggling to pay bills he hadn't had to worry about at Roundway, Walrond passionately immersed himself in research for the program, delving into archives at the British Museum and crafting an ambitious plan for the show, as well as compiling a companion anthology, complete with an original ten-thousand-word essay. Finally, a potential path back into the literary world! Indeed, the work did help precipitate reunions with some luminaries from his past, including W.E.B. Du Bois and Langston Hughes. But the project proved complicated, riddled with false starts, funding hurdles, and fickle publishers. It seems Walrond was unable, for whatever reason, to deliver on his grand designs. Maybe it was the scale of the task, larger than anything he'd attempted for a long time; maybe it was that familiar death knell, the pressure to succeed, for this might be his last chance.

Sadly, the plan for the anthology fell apart, and Walrond fell off to the margins of the project. Still, the performance, *Black and Unknown Bards*, eventually went ahead at London's Royal Court Theatre, for one night only, in October 1958, as Britain was reeling from the Notting Hill race riots. The press praised its potency and relevance.

"At a time when it is particularly necessary to draw attention to the talent, dignity, sufferings and aspirations of the coloured peoples, we have this excellent programme which does just that," wrote *The Daily Worker*. Despite the internal difficulties, the production bore Walrond's imprint. I'd like to think he permitted himself to take pride in it.

It did not, however, secure his place in London's literary scene. Almost sixty years old by this point, he once again found himself in a financially precarious position, struggling to see writing projects through and despondent as a result. Correspondence from the period reveals that he was trailed by shame and anguish that his life had amounted to far less than what it was supposed to. Desperate for work, he took a job at an export packing firm, while his health deteriorated. In 1966, at age sixty-seven, he met his end— a heart attack on the street, alone.

Eric Walrond's life was one of dislocation, movement, and change, churned by the waves of history. Of crossing borders, falling into unfamiliar worlds, falling out of them. Writing boldly throughout, demonstrating, however sporadically, a dedication to his subject and craft, despite having published only one book. Had Walrond not experienced that early, sharp ascent, that flicker of fame, his career might have been considered a modest success. But the narrative of rise and fizzle is limned with tragedy. There are so many reasons why Walrond—labeled "promising," "brilliant," and a "genius" by so many—didn't become a household name, didn't "live up to" the mandate that he was destined for greatness.

Mental health struggles. Racial barriers. Lack of strategy. A volatile personality. Loneliness. Fate. Bad luck. Or perhaps he wasn't so great, after all. It's easy to proclaim someone great, but hard to be the person who actually has to achieve greatness. Perhaps, as many of his onetime friends theorized, he undermined himself by leaving New York when he was most successful. He had all the pieces arranged, he was in the right place at the right time—the epicenter of Black culture in America—he'd been noticed, he was poised for liftoff… and he ran away.

Or, he was just doing what he felt like doing. Responding, perhaps, to an inner restlessness, a feeling, forged in his multilocational childhood, of comfort in being on the outskirts, in a place marked by some sort of self-dissonance. In Guiana, a Barbadian. In Barbados, a Brit. In Panama, a West Indian. In New York, a Caribbean. In England, an American. It seemed that the brief window when he was the next big thing in New York, when he had gotten into the in-crowd, was precisely when he started to feel uneasy, to feel a need to flee, seek the edge, seek elsewhere. "What attracts me is elsewhere, and I don't know where that elsewhere is," writes Emil Cioran, and I wonder if Walrond felt that too. I certainly do. I find his story compelling because I see echoes of myself in Walrond, and echoes of many people I know, whether or not we published acclaimed books when we were in our twenties. I left a comfortable, supportive milieu because I became restless, because stability wasn't enough, because—even if it meant a kind of self-sabotage, a casting off of a world that could potentially lift me up—I needed to go in search of that elsewhere on my own.

I often think the world is made up of two types of people: searchers and stayers. Searchers are guided by a fundamental restlessness, an underlying preference for movement over stillness, change over consistency. They tend to continually reinvent themselves, trying on new personas, styles, mediums, jobs, genres, religions, routines, ways of being. They root sideways rather than down, choose breadth rather than depth. I'm not suggesting one is better than the other. Stayers are more likely to commit, to focus, to stick to it and be rewarded for their perseverance. Stayers are perhaps better at sublimating a desire for novelty in favor of throwing themselves wholeheartedly into one thing. Stayers, motivated by concreteness and security, are perhaps more likely to build something lasting. I'd venture to say that stayers write more books.

I believe Walrond is, in many ways, an archetype, with a path shared by many a searcher. Consider, for example, the little-known poet–painter–collagist–novelist–playwright–lamp designer–gallerist–socialite Mina Loy. Born to Hungarian Jewish and English parents in London in 1882 as Mina Lowy (she dropped the *w* in her early twenties), Loy was a key participant in nearly every major Western artistic movement of the twentieth century, from futurist Florence to Freudian Vienna to surrealist Paris to modernist New York. In expat Florence, she socialized with Gertrude Stein, Alice B. Toklas, André Gide. In New York, she was friends with Man Ray, Marcel Duchamp, Joseph Cornell. She designed lamps with Peggy Guggenheim. She acted in plays with William Carlos Williams. Her poetry was admired by T. S. Eliot. In a letter to Marianne Moore, Ezra Pound wrote: "Is there anyone in America except you, Bill [William Carlos Williams], and Mina Loy who can write anything of interest in verse?" So many admirers, so many affiliations with today's household names, so much praise and promise—and yet she published just two books of poetry in her lifetime. She disappeared to Aspen, Colorado, in her later years. Her one novel, *Insel*—written in the mid-1930s, about a charged relationship between a German painter and an American art dealer in bohemian Paris—didn't see publication until 1991, a quarter century after her death, when interest in this largely unknown yet seemingly central figure of the modernist movement started to pick up. Why, having been at the heart of so many scenes, possessing such demonstrable gifts, did she, at least according to a linear rubric of fame, not amount to much? Why does she instead dwell in the category of the "forgotten" or "overlooked"? One explanation is that, not unlike Walrond, she kept leaving the worlds she so easily seemed to fall into. Her voracious creative appetite meant that she kept reinventing her calling, sampling new mediums and identities. And she was doomed to be good at everything she tried. Perhaps she had a kind of addiction to mastering one domain and then moving on, to always being on the verge of novelty, to searching rather than staying. Had she stuck with one thing, maybe her name would be more decisively etched into the canon today. But that would have required her to be a different person.

The life of American satirical novelist and short-story writer Dawn Powell is another version of the Walrond archetype. A transplant from rural Ohio to New York in the 1920s, she found her way into the Greenwich Village arts scene and earned the admiration and friendship of Ernest Hemingway (she was, apparently, his "favorite living writer") and E. E. Cummings for her comedic and acerbic social critiques, particularly of life in New York ("delicate and cutting—nothing will cut New York but a diamond" is the kind of work she hoped to produce). Though she was widely praised by critics, and continually rubbed shoulders with the literati, she struggled financially and failed to earn a living from writing. She didn't epically flop or stratospherically succeed; hers was a life lived on that spectrum of winning and losing, of taking off and not taking off. One reason may be that, like Walrond, she was ahead of her time in terms of style and subject matter. During her lifetime, her harsh satires—full of sharp observations and uncomfortable truths, lampooning millionaires and communists alike—didn't sell well, perhaps because they hit everyone too close to home. But posthumously—with endorsements from the likes of Gore Vidal, Rory from *Gilmore Girls*, and Tim Page, who called her "one of America's greatest writers"—her body of work gleams with enduring relevance. Still, she's more famous for not being famous than for the writing that, for better or for worse, steered the course of her life.

And then there's Henry Roth, a Jewish immigrant to New York who, in 1934, published *Call It Sleep*, a novel about a young boy growing up in the bleak environs of the Lower East Side tenements. Cue discussion of the author's singular gifts, exceptional promise, great potential. Cue critical acclaim from important magazines of the day. Lewis Gannett, writing in the *New York Herald Tribune*, predicted that anyone who read it would "remember it and talk about it and watch excitedly" for Roth's next book. What followed, instead, was more than three decades of writer's block for Roth, during which time he sidled out of New York and worked as a road laborer, a substitute math teacher, an attendant at a mental hospital, a duck and goose farmer, and a precision tool grinder, among other things. Why did his writing fizzle out? Again, the possible explanations are manifold. Perhaps the weight of expectation was too great, crippling any sense of artistic freedom; the longer he didn't write, the more the ghosts of failure haunted him. Perhaps his personal life was too complicated, his political beliefs too confusing, his mind too mercurial, his childhood too troubled. Perhaps he was predisposed to capriciousness. Perhaps he was just living his life, intuitively and nonstrategically, letting it unfold, as most of us do, in the only way he knew how. In 1964, thirty years after its first publication, *Call It Sleep* was republished as an overlooked Depression-era masterpiece, and went on to sell over a million copies. This second wave of success helped ease Roth, who was living on a farm in Maine, out of his writer's block, though it took him a few more decades to complete his second book, a monumental four-volume novel. The first installment of *Mercy of a Rude Stream* was published sixty-two years after his debut. Would more consistent success

# THE ROBBERY

*by Natalie Eilbert*

The story goes the man waited until the customers
cleared the bank before robbing it. He hoped to be caught,

because he struggled with his health and needed health care
the prison would provide. A plea hearing in May, facing

40 years. The world hurts all over, the ground a circuit of vessels
stamped into bruise. Someone emails me to correct my word choice,

uses the Holocaust as an example, in case it helps to learn
by example. I walk zero miles today, disappear briefly into

sleep, my nothingness gentle, like meltwater trapped in quartz.
I don't fear death. The story goes that he chose a young bank teller,

did his best to not scare him. The man took $1,700 from the teller,
the man waited in his car for the blue lights of police cars. Maybe

he listened to an Eagles song. Maybe rain made slick the hoarfrost.
Maybe steam rose briefly from dirty ice mounds. A cavalry of finches

perched outside my balcony as the highway droned like a sideways
heaven half dug into earth. God, I don't know what to do with this life.

---

have given us a different Henry Roth? "There was another life that I might have had," Kazuo Ishiguro once said, "but I am having this one."

There are lives lived on the verge of taking off, somewhere in the orbit of success and failure, striving, hoping, subject to the whims of all manner of external forces. And then there is the inverse. A friend who used to teach poetry at a prestigious university recently told me about a student of his who, in all his years as a professor, was a singular standout. He was completely blown away by the strangeness and confidence of her language, her phenomenally original voice, her ability to produce, week after week, intricately cut and brilliantly polished gems that left the class speechless, wonderstruck. Just as incredible was this student's complete nonchalance about her talent. Having seen hundreds of students sail unremarkably through his poetry seminars, my friend was sure he had a genius on his hands, the next Emily Dickinson (who, lest we forget, was unknown in her lifetime), or, at the very least, H.D. (another Walrond-esque case study, who was crowned great when she was young but died in obscurity, only to be canonized later). Anyway, upon this student's graduation, he urged her to apply for fellowships and MFAs, to submit her work to contests, to frequent certain institutions—to, essentially, do the "right things." She moved to New York and they loosely stayed in touch. After a couple of years, they met up, and my friend eagerly asked about her writing. "I've forgotten how," she said, without revealing any trace of longing or remorse. She'd taken up a job as a technical writer for a nonprofit; she had a boyfriend. She seemed content.

My friend was stunned, confused, disappointed—how could she not want more, not want to at least try? But maybe she didn't want to. Certainly there's something admirable, indeed enviable, about that effortless detachment from one's gifts. The cool "I've forgotten how," in this instance, makes this young person even more alluring. Not only is she brilliant, she doesn't give a fuck! She's not even going to do anything about it! It's often the smartest ones who don't. We all know someone like that, the shadow genius, either uninterested in or unable to get their act together, their brilliance amplified by the fact that they're not utilizing it. Said James Baldwin: "I know a lot of talented ruins."

I'd like to believe, in the case of my friend's former student, that her actions reflect a genuine, deep contentment, a Zen-like sublimation of the ego. But that's only one explanation. Perhaps she *is* secretly agonizing over what she isn't doing. Perhaps it's a defensive posture, a shield against the prospect of future artistic failure. Perhaps it's her teacher's benefaction backfiring—in pronouncing her great, he smothered her ability to produce, and she collapsed under the weight of expectation. Perhaps, in five years' time, or ten, or twenty, she will want more, and she'll find it harder to get, having missed the earlier boat. The irreverence of "I've forgotten how" might be recast as writer's block; the freedom associated with *not* doing something you're good at might, later on, feel like wasted time. Who knows. When you're young, you can be flippant about your promise, because that's all you are. Having done nothing, you can enjoy the prospect of anything. But life is often long.

Eric Walrond was not particularly flippant about his promise—he knew he had it, and he wanted to use it—although he did make decisions that, in hindsight, might be described as self-defeating. Why didn't he ride the wave of attention when he had it? Why did he leave New York, and his milieu of famous friends, at the height of his success? Rather than sink deeper into that world, he rose out of it. He floated across the sea to another place, another milieu, another scene, where he repeatedly created himself anew. He didn't stop trying, but he didn't quite find his anchor again. What would have happened had he stayed put?

I think of another friend of mine, a musician from a small Western nation. After playing in decently successful bands in his twenties, he released a debut solo album that was extolled by the press, landed him gigs at significant venues around the world, won him a major national prize, and basically positioned him to do whatever he wanted to do next. Instead, as opportunities flowed his way, he quietly made a second album, which, apart from personally giving a few copies to friends, he chose not to release publicly. "But why not?" everyone pressed. His answer: "I didn't want to talk about it." He couldn't face the prospect of discussing the turmoil that had turned into lyrics, of providing tidy anecdotes to explain his arrangements. Years later, he hasn't reentered the music world. He is working at a greengrocer. He has become a shadow genius, glorified—whether he wants it or not—by the glow of opting out.

"I didn't want to talk about it." Another elegant refusal, akin to "I've forgotten how." What's with these people? Have they reached enlightenment? I want to think that their inaction speaks to something like that: a deep wisdom, a fundamental understanding that artistic recognition isn't all it's cracked up to be, a profound internal peace. External validation is a trap! Don't you know what happens when you get what you want? You want more. Yeah, yeah, the hedonic treadmill. We all know this, but they *really* know it. They know that in the end—regardless of how sublime the actual work of creativity is, all the stuff that comes after, if you're lucky to receive it—all the packaging and performing and selling and feting and traveling and talking just might not be worth it. The poet knew it before she even started. The musician had a taste of it, and then spit it out.

Or maybe there's something else going on. Maybe they're afraid. Or lazy. Or boring. Whatever the explanation, opting out is not for everyone. *Imagine*, one might retort, *being so lucky as to be able to turn down opportunities!* Check your privilege, you sages. Strivers of the world, unite! Why choose equanimity when you can ride the roller coaster of external validation? The lows are low, but the highs are oh so, so high. Not everyone has to be a Buddhist, right? To each their own.

While writing this essay, an artifact from years ago wandered into my mind: a list I made with a friend in a college dorm room at 2 a.m., circa 2009, titled "Top 25 People You Should Know at [our liberal arts university]." It was our snarky yet studied assessment of the sparkliest people on campus, the experimental thespians and the a cappella divas and the EDM bros and the spoken-word stars, the ones who we thought were really going somewhere. Thankfully, it never saw the light of day, but without much effort, I was able to find it on an old hard drive, tucked between essays on the theatre of the oppressed and transcendentalism.

It is a hilarious document. Instantly, I'm transported back to the college green. Skinny jeans proliferate. Merriweather Post Pavilion drifts through the air. I go down the list and google. One person has become a famous musician. Another, a well-known poet. Another acts in buzzy TV shows. These people have Wikipedia pages. Others indicate occasional creative output—a YouTube clip from a 2013 standup gig, a chapbook prize in 2015, a 2017 personal essay—in and around creative-adjacent professions like brand strategist. A few are employed as therapists and social workers. There are some surprises: a campus heartthrob has gone into medicine; a charismatic dancer has dropped out in South America. In fact, the majority yield very little online. A mention at the end of a parent's obituary, a password-protected wedding website, a lapsed LinkedIn. Two on the list are dead.

The spread is characteristic, I suppose, of any cohort, any scene, any group of friends. A couple of triumphs, a couple of tragedies, and most everyone else just… swimming along, living lives that are probably some ever-shifting combination of thrilling and repetitive, frustrating and satisfying, quiet and loud, ordinary and extraordinary. Inevitably, disparities of a certain kind of success widen over time; people fall off; the refrain *Whatever happened to so-and-so?* begins to resound. It happened in Walrond's Harlem Renaissance–era crew; it happened in Mina Loy's downtown scene; it'll happen to us. We all know people who are slipping through the cracks; maybe we ourselves are those people. Some among us who found early success might struggle, in a few years, to sustain it. Some among us might experience a meteoric rise tomorrow. Some among us might fail spectacularly in three decades. Most of us, though, will probably just keep trying and not trying, hoping and not hoping, changing and not changing, stepping forward and falling backward, somewhere in the vast, variegated experiment that is, simply, life.

Storylines of artistic success tend to adhere to a few templates. There's the narrative of steady upward movement, the "Sea-to-Summit," let us call it, whereby talent and perseverance are rewarded with professional acclaim and canonical recognition at a rate that steadily increases over the course of one's lifetime. There's a life spent toiling in bitter obscurity, only to score a late break and enjoy a whirlwind third act of glamour and glory: "Waiting for Godot," but vindicated. Then there's "Future Queen," the hermetic, unknown genius whose prolific output is posthumously wrested from the rubble and propelled to household-name status. Or there's the beloved tale of youthful fame and early, untimely death, the "Rocket to Heaven," say, its subject forever bathed in the tragic yet ennobling glow of unfulfilled potential. Of course, real lives are never this neat, but these are the cinematic arcs, the ones deemed worthy of biopics.

What we don't have is a template for an arc like Walrond's. Someone who

could have been any of the above, but who instead meandered, on a rutted, twisting road, sometimes succeeding, sometimes failing, most of the time inhabiting the space between those reductive poles. Whose trajectory is not linear, not straightforwardly tragic or triumphant, but complex, bittersweet—like most of our journeys are. Trajectories of success, as Walrond's story demonstrates, are usually at odds with the vicissitudes of life, and the restlessness and changeability that tend to define creative people. In that sense, for me, Walrond is a blueprint for a life lived honestly, vulnerably, on the raw edge of what it means to be human. His choices were intuitive, searching, responsive to the inclinations of his soul. He seemed to follow his heart—however confounding or nonstrategic that might have been. He was unerringly, unapologetically, himself.

One-hit wonder. Fifteen minutes of fame. Flavor of the month. Second-book syndrome. There's even homo unius libri—man of one book, attributed to Thomas Aquinas. Our vocabulary for artists who flame out is limited, pejorative. The terms we turn to are more indictments of industries that fetishize novelty than verdicts on an artist's capacity to sustain an output. In the end, it's all a bit of a toss-up, even if we'd prefer to think otherwise, to believe that those destined for greatness will, in fact, become great. As Tom Bissell writes, "I cannot help but imagine that literature is an airplane, and we passengers on it. One might assume that behind the flimsy accordion door sit pilots of skill and accomplishment. But the cockpit is empty. It has always been empty. The controls are abandoned. They have always been abandoned. One needs only to touch them to know how mutable our course." And if literary fame is random, literary failure is just as random. There are infinite reasons why—even if they've been anointed great, even if they have the right connections, the right timing, the right smarts, the right mystique—some people do not reach the heights set out before them. Walrond's path was marked by particular, undeniable struggles. Who he was (an immigrant from the Caribbean, navigating, among other things, colonialism and racial regimes) and who he became (a charming and brilliant but troubled person) had as much to do with his success as with his failure. A writer today might encounter similar as well as different issues: an inability to use Instagram, an oversaturated market, the cultural devaluing of the arts, the encroachment of technology, a world driven by the financial imperatives of corporations, et cetera, et cetera. The banquet of obstacles is always lavish. Though maybe we've reached a point in history when none of us will have time to fizzle out; instead, we'll be cleanly, dramatically swallowed by artificial intelligence, rendered extinct, the last of the species once known as artists. That would be cinematic.

In the meantime, however, I propose we celebrate not just the stories of the against-all-odds successes, the posthumous geniuses, the Sea-to-Summits, but also the quiet, smoldering grandeur of lives that are shaped the other way. Those who, like Eric Walrond, keep searching, climbing, ambulating through the hills of that vast middle—even if they never quite make it to Mount Nebo.

This is what I think as I stand before Walrond's mud-splattered grave this afternoon—five winters on from our first encounter, after a hailstorm has whipped through London—in the warmth of a late-breaking sun. A promised land never fully glimpsed, a hunger never entirely satiated. Moments of joy, beauty, and possibility scattered throughout, accessible even through the hardship, poignant in their transience. It's a different sort of cinematic, a different sort of admirable. You can feel it in the first pages of *Tropic Death*:

> Hunger—pricks at stomachs inured to brackish coffee and cassava pone—pressed on folk, joyful as rabbits in a grassy ravine, wrenching themselves free of the lure of the white earth. Helter-skelter dark, brilliant, black faces of West Indian peasants moved along, in pain—the stiff tails of blue denim coats, the hobble of chigger-cracked heels, the rhythm of a stride... dissipating into the sun-stuffed void the radiant forces of the incline.

And you can feel it in the words Walrond wrote, close to the end, to those who once believed in him:

> I am determined to try somehow and get on with some of my own, long-neglected work... I have only one thing to live for, and in spite of age and years of silence I have not lost sight of my objectives, or the high aims with which I set out such a long time ago. ★

THE TRUE STORY OF A NOVELIST CAUGHT UP IN THE
PRISON SYSTEM OF AN AUTHORITARIAN REGIME

A FINALIST FOR THE 2023

# NATIONAL BOOK CRITICS CIRCLE AWARD

*for* AUTOBIOGRAPHY

"A moving testament to the power of free expression. It's tough to forget."

—*Publishers Weekly*

"Ahmed Naji confronts what happens when one's fundamentally unserious, oversexed youth dovetails with an authoritarian, utterly self-serious regime."

—Zadie Smith, author of *The Fraud*

"A top-tier work of prison literature."

—*Foreword Reviews*, starred review

"A tragicomedy stripped down to its last nerve."

—Noor Naga, author of
*If an Egyptian Cannot Speak English*

ROTTEN EVIDENCE

AHMED NAJI

TRANSLATED BY KATHARINE HALLS

# HERNAN DIAZ

[WRITER]

"CAN YOU IMAGINE BEING SURE OF YOUR
WRITING ALL THE TIME? WHAT A HORRIBLE
WORLD THAT WOULD BE."

How Hernan Diaz writes a great novel:
*He sets rules*
*He does it for the love of the sentence*
*He trusts the audience—and asks the*
*audience to trust him*

*H*ernan Diaz leaped into our collective literary consciousness with both feet via his 2017 debut, In the Distance, *a revisionist western tale of a gentle Swedish emigrant meandering through the hardships and violence of the American Old West in search of his lost brother. The book was a finalist for the PEN/Faulkner Award for Fiction and the Pulitzer Prize, the latter of which Diaz secured for his second novel,* Trust. *An onion of a book,* Trust *begins with the story of a 1920s Wall Street tycoon, then progressively peels back narrative layers to expose the voices of those silenced by capital, patriarchy, and power. Born, raised, and educated in Argentina, Sweden, and London before settling in New York, Diaz peppers his work with elements relevant to an unanchored life: Plenty of loneliness and cultural isolation. Diverse perspectives. A longing for home and comfort that never quite manifests. An impulse toward justice, paralleled by pragmatism regarding the all-too-frequent frustration of it.*

69

*This is my second interview with Diaz—both by way of Zoom—and I know from our previous conversation that he grew up viewing the United States from afar, on a basis of "fictional experience," gleaning his awareness of American culture through cinema, literature, and music. By now, his writing has been woven into that cultural mythos, so far contributing to the exploration of two of the most American of narratives: those of the western wanderer and the consummate capitalist. He turns both these archetypes on their heads, perhaps benefiting from the removed vantage afforded by a cosmopolitan existence. There is a special sort of objectivity that comes with being from a little bit of everywhere and a little bit of nowhere.*

*Abiding in Diaz's fiction is an almost academic sense of analytic detachment, though that is not to say it lacks vitality. Quite the opposite. While he writes with a cool, scientific discipline—like an archaeologist patiently digging up, then piecing together the bits of some long-lost people—this investigative framework is fleshed out with ample poetics, occasional humor, and something akin to magnanimity. It is not without good reason that his novels have garnered such acclaim. These are works of a serious and skillful author, artist, and auditor of the human condition.*

*—Nick Hilden*

### I. "WITHOUT A SHOT BEING FIRED"

THE BELIEVER: So I had just finished re-reading *In the Distance* and written the note "*In the Distance* feels like *Blood Meridian*, but the opposite." Then, ten minutes later, an alert popped up that Cormac McCarthy had died. Was he an influence on you? Were you a fan?

HERNAN DIAZ: Of course I was a fan—well, no, let's strike that; I hate the word *fan*. I don't like that word or the fact that it stems from *fanaticism* and this unconditional allegiance to something or someone. I dislike it, so let's start over. Yes, I've read a lot of Cormac McCarthy. He really was a massive inspiration in regard to how to approach the western from an angle that was new and wasn't fully part of the canon. I always both admired and was made a little insane by aspects of his prose. Especially his idiosyncratic punctuation, which sometimes is a source of joy and sometimes is a source of irritation, because I really see punctuation on the page.

But *Blood Meridian* is probably the most important novel for me of the McCarthy books I've read. I remember being overwhelmed by its violence in a way I've seldom been. Just the feeling of being hit by the book. It's almost a Nietzschean western, and it got me thinking a lot. I read it before I put pen to paper on *In the Distance*, and it's a massively important book for me.

BLVR: The literature of the American Old West tends to overtly or at least implicitly glorify violence. But your western—although there is violence, it's almost a reaction against it. When Håkan commits acts of violence, he abhors it. Would you say you were trying consciously to react against these tropes, or did that come naturally as you wrote it?

HD: Once I decided to set the novel in the American West, and in that particular period of time, I knew I would have to delve into the ossified perception we have of that era. That includes the aestheticized and romantic view of violence. Usually this romantic view of violence and of the heroic gunslinger is tied in with a deep-seated suspicion of institutions and the state. It's this vigilante who is righting wrongs outside an institutional framework, even if that means going against the law and the embodiment of the law—the vigilante against the corrupt sheriff.

Because of this lawless or paralegal justice—even better, "supra-legal" justice—there is a notion of justice that is above the letter of the law. The enforcement of this kind of justice is always done through violence. This is one of the reasons why violence is so important. Another reason is because of the genocidal drive that lies behind the western. Let's not forget that the push west comes with the extermination of the native peoples who were there. Also of the flora and fauna that were replaced by intensive agriculture. Just think about it: "cowboys"—it's all about cows, but there were no cows native to the West. That's an industrial introduction of an animal at the expense of other animals, mostly buffalo. The cowboy is a sign of domestication and of how this space was disciplined. There is a violence against other peoples, there is a violence against fellow human beings in general, and there is a violence against the environment, which is now deemed a source for the extraction of capital for the incipient Industrial Revolution. So, yes, I very much wanted to address this.

But I confess that when I first put pen to paper, I considered dropping the whole project, because I knew that the book relied on that violent scene with Håkan. I knew that scene had to be there, but I didn't want to write it. The plot from that point on is motivated by that scene, because Håkan goes into exile as a result of it. He's broken and devastated by the violence he has committed. The book abounds very deliberately in clichés from the genre, and it opens almost immediately with a classic showdown. I told myself, If I can solve this showdown without a single shot being fired, then perhaps I can write the book. That was the test I set for myself. I did indeed write the showdown without a shot being fired, and off I went. The one big violent scene—there are two, I think; the biggest one in which Håkan is involved—I wrote almost in one sitting, feeling really bad about it.

BLVR: You brought up the treatment of Indigenous people and Native Americans. I've been reading David Graeber's last book, in which he discusses the historical infantilization of native peoples and the tendency to portray them as naive creatures living in nature. You show them more as he suggests: as complicated people who have a science of their own, who have a medicine of their own. This old medicine man teaches Håkan important things. I really appreciated that, because of this tendency of the western genre to infantilize different native peoples. When you were writing about Native American culture, were you being imaginative or were you doing research? How did you go about that?

HD: I was doing both those things. I was trying to be responsible and do archival work and read as much as I could. But it's also a work of the imagination. Both those elements were also amalgamated for the Scandinavian immigrant and for the pioneers in the caravan on the trail. It's always an alloy of research and imagination, and I am always trying to do it as carefully and mindfully and respectfully as I can. But I think research should always be a means toward imagining things more sharply rather than a way of corseting imagination. When you are depicting a group that is not necessarily yours, you should always ask yourself why you're doing it, how you're doing it, from what perspective you're doing it, and be really serious and ethically conscientious.

I should also say that when I finish a project, I leave that world behind for a while. I haven't really revisited any of the western materials or that world. And now that I'm done with *Trust*, I haven't been reading about money, you know, because my mind is elsewhere and I'm trying to find a new thing. It feels weird to be a visitor in a world that for a while was mine.

## II. REFERENTIAL FETISHISM

BLVR: In *In the Distance* you describe the desert beautifully. Did you spend much time there as a visitor?

HD: I'm almost Oulipian in private, quirky, personal ways that are meaningless to people other than me. I set weird rules for myself. Sometimes I don't realize they are in place until I'm confronted with them over and over again. With *In the Distance*, one very overt rule was that I'm not going to go and have an air-conditioned experience of those spaces from, like, a Ford Focus or whatever. [*Laughter*] It didn't seem to make any sense at all to me. Elsewhere I've written on this notion of "referential fetishism." It's something I try to avoid at all costs. I defend the notion of literature as, ultimately, a product of literature itself that, to a large extent, mirrors other literature. Not necessarily as the vehicle for referential accuracy. There are other discourses and genres that do that much better, if that's what you're after. Perfect mimesis—that's not why I read fiction.

With *In the Distance* I did two things. First, I gave myself all the space I needed to imagine these places. Then the second thing I did was to read a lot about them: mostly primary materials from the time. I read a lot of travel writing like Francis Parkman, who, weirdly, was reviewed by Melville—and destroyed by Melville, actually, when it comes to Parkman's violently racist depiction of Native Americans. Richard Henry Dana, John Muir, guides to gold mines for prospectors, how-to manuals from the mid-nineteenth century. That's the stuff I read, and somehow it made that territory more vivid in my mind than being there. Does that make sense?

BLVR: Absolutely. We were talking about Cormac McCarthy earlier, and in *Blood Meridian*, he describes them as these alien landscapes, and they don't look like that. His fever dream of it is more interesting than the reality.

HD: I could piggyback on that and say I think the western as a genre—also in film—exoticizes America for Americans. If you look at John Ford's movies, they're all shot essentially in the same location—what is it, Monument Valley?—over and over again. That's obviously implausible. Talk about going against referential fetishization, accuracy, mimesis. That's all out the window from the first exterior shot. These films are about something else. They're about, to a certain extent, the clichéd and hyper-calcified view we have of these places, which tops any other referential aspiration. Think of Sergio Leone's spaghetti westerns. They're all shot in Almería, Spain. They just have to convey western-ness. Not even west-ness, but western-ness. I think that is the main thing for that particular genre, where landscape plays such a massive role. The archetype, however hyperbolic, distorted, or even fake it may be, is way more important than the real thing.

BLVR: Upon re-reading *In the Distance*, one thing that struck me as both heartbreaking and wonderful was the decision to not allow Håkan to reencounter Linus. You have this scene in your mind that maybe the long-lost brothers… but you withhold that satisfaction. Was that a decision you made going in, or did that come out of the process?

HD: I was talking about the Oulipian rules I set for myself. Another such rule was that—and this is actually expressed in a sentence that occurs in some shape in the last quarter of the novel—the protagonist would never be able to retrieve anything he had left behind. He would never be able to go back to a place he had been to before. The only exception to this was when he went back to the mining town.

BLVR: But it's all changed.

HD: It's all changed. It's not even that town anymore. It could well be a different place altogether. The only thing that's the same is the geographical location. So that was the rule: always forward. It was a hard rule to follow. Many narrative junctures and issues with the mechanics of the plot would have been much more easily solved without that rule, but I stuck with it. Of course, not being able to find his brother is part of that rule. At the end of the day, this is a book about radical loneliness. It's not a book about

communion, reunion, or reconciliation. It's a novel about a very final form of loneliness. To have that reencounter at the end would have been an utter betrayal of what the book was trying to convey.

### III. "THE COLD, DARK SHADOW OF UNIVERSAL REJECTION"

BLVR: The last time we spoke, you mentioned that back around the 2008 financial crisis, you'd written a first book that never got published. What was that book like? Was it completed?

HD: Totally finished. It's a novel that *almost* got published a bunch of times and never did. It's a reasonable step in whatever path these books seem to be making. It deals with a lot of the themes that seem to come up over and over again. It's about loneliness, the United States, immigration, in a weird way. There's a lot there that is a blueprint for what I did after. And there are so many other texts that never saw the light of day.

BLVR: When you published *In the Distance*, you didn't have an agent, and you went straight through a small press, and it was a finalist for the Pulitzer Prize. Then *Trust* found a very eager audience and ultimately won the Pulitzer. Were you surprised by the receptiveness that both novels received?

HD: Yes, because I had been writing for a really long time in the cold, dark shadow of universal rejection. Nobody would touch my stuff. So of course it was really—and it keeps being—very joyful and very strange. I don't take anything for granted, being a middle-aged person who has devoted his entire life to reading and writing, for the most part in solitude. So this is… this is great.

BLVR: Was it frustrating before people recognized your work?

HD: Of course. I wish I had that fortitude and extreme devotion and resolution that would lead to not caring at all. I would be writing even if it were with evanescent ink, even if by the end of the page everything was gone, I would still do it. You know? I'm not quite there; I believe in literature as a conversation, and that requires interlocutors. I won't lie—it really hurt to be told to stop. That was the message I was getting from the world: just *please stop*. It's weird because you feel very lonely, but if you love to do this thing, you keep doing it, and that creates a very dangerous, solipsistic kind of state of mind where you feel your opinion is the only thing you have to sustain your work. That's not a very healthy place. It is maddening. In every possible sense of that word, it is maddening. So those were not happy times. But whatever solace I found, I did find in the joy of inhabiting language, which is why I do this. Doing it for any other reason is insane. There has to be at least some willingness to write with that evanescent ink. There has to be some of that in you.

BLVR: As a writer myself, and in talking to lots of writers, I find there's this kind of split personality to being a writer where, on one hand, you have to be almost psychotically confident in your writing to expect people to pay you for it. You have to have the confidence to say, *I don't care about rejection, and I will do it again and again and get rejected again and again.* But then at the same time, once you finally do start selling, once you finally do get whatever success looks like, there's this impostor syndrome that sets in. So you go through this crazy cycle of insane confidence followed by impostor syndrome.

HD: I don't think about it that way. Everything I've written, I've written alone. I finish it and I discuss it with very few people. My wife, in the first place, who is also my first and most excellent reader and a massive influence. But other than that, I don't share chapters with my agent. I don't share drafts with my editor. Also, I don't write drafts. I don't pitch short stories to magazines. I just write a thing. And the market (to somehow name the sum of those objective forces) is of no consideration. This is in response to what you just said: *I'm writing this and you will pay me for it.* I'm not trying to be precious or presumptuous about it. I'm telling you truly how it works for me. I write something— a short story, a full novel—and nobody except for, again, a very small group of very close people sees it. And when it's done, now that I have an agent (a relatively new development), I give it to him. And then,

I don't know, we talk and we see what happens. Is it viable? There is no commercial target I'm trying to hit. There is no buyer for anything I'm writing, ever. Later, of course, I am invested in the whole process because it's my job and I have a child and a mortgage. It's not that I'm above all that, but I don't write toward it. About the impostor syndrome, I think being a bit afraid, uncomfortable, out of your depth is absolutely essential. Can you imagine being sure of your writing all the time? What a horrible world that would be. What I want is lucid doubt.

### IV. "A DENT IN HISTORY"

BLVR: When you write a book like *Trust*, which takes some pretty big structural, narrative risks, you really have to have a lot of trust in your audience that they're going to go along with it. You were just saying you don't really show your work to people. So when you were working on *Trust*, were you worried that people wouldn't follow that narrative, or was it something you were confident about?

HD: There were some points I was worried about. And, thank you, you're the first, weirdly, to mention that *Trust*, the title, also refers to trust—it could be taken to be a verb in the imperative mood: you, comma, trust me or the book. Which is definitely a semantic layer I was going for. The first thing that worried me is that the second section is written in this very abrasive, macho tone, and it abounds in pseudo-technical financial jargon. It was very important for me to have that voice: it has been screaming at us from history books and newspapers forever. I wanted to re-create that voice and then underpin it. It's also a major plot point: you have this very loud male voice, and then you find out that it's actually the creation of this young woman, this writer who made this voice up, who made this monster up. *Frankenstein* is a big influence for me, always. So that's why that had to be there. This comes after the first section, which is a whole novel within the novel, written in what I think (hope) is a terse, highly stylized, and polished sort of tone. Maybe I've failed, but that's what I was going for.

In the second part, however, you can feel the cogwheels of this very clunky, aggressive prose. It was so long, and I thought, I can't live with this voice for a year, which is what it would have taken to write, like, 150 pages of that. Man, I thought, I can't subject readers to 150 pages of this. So that's when I decided to shatter that section, smash it, and have this kind of textual shrapnel, which gave it a formal edge that, to me, made it way more interesting. Each page in that section is typeset with extreme care. My editor was very patient with me, so line breaks and page breaks really fall in very specific places to create certain effects. Many of them are quite humorous, hopefully in a quiet, discreet way. That fragmentation ended up contracting the whole thing in a way I found appealing. But I was still worried. As I said, we come from this very stylized and sort of almost lush prose at times, and then there is this aggressive thing. Like, we build this capital of goodwill with the reader, and then we just burn through it in about five pages. Then the task is to build it again, to start again. That's where the trust you mentioned, the trust in the reader, comes in.

BLVR: Obviously, *Trust* is largely about the erasure of women's narratives. Does a writer have a responsibility to expose lost narratives or ignored narratives or oppressed narratives?

HD: This Sartrean notion of commitment or responsibility feels very alien to me. I don't believe that literature should be subordinated to anything other than beauty, emotion, fairness, and the ethics of the storytelling itself. I think storytelling is profoundly ethical because it has to do with a certain form of knowledge and how that knowledge is presented and administered. In that regard, it also involves another person—the reader—toward whom I feel I have a responsibility. The reader is someone I don't want to cheat. I don't want to pull a fast one on anyone. I also don't want to be unfair to my characters. That is a very important thing to me, to never be a jerk, even if the characters themselves are jerks. [*Laughter*]

Of course there is the obligation, to my mind, of writing something moving. If there isn't that emotional dimension, I'm out. There's no purpose for me. But also raw emotion, just howling on the page, is not something I personally am interested in. That brings in the third element that I just mentioned, which is a certain sense of formal rigor and control and discipline and elegance that I associate with that elusive quality we call "beauty." Perhaps literature is the result of the triangulation of these vertices: emotion, formal rigor, and ethical responsibility. I do, of course, feel it is important to recover silenced voices, and I think my work speaks to that. You asked me if this was an imperative of literature as a whole, and that's where I don't necessarily… It has been an imperative for *me*. But there's so much literature that I love where that doesn't play a major role, and I still love that literature, and I defend that literature even if it doesn't do that. I get a little worried when literature is subordinated to something that is extra-literary, because I think that sets it on a path that turns it into yet another instrumental device in a hyper-instrumentalized society.

BLVR: Recently in the United States there has been a rising tide of bans and opposition to books that portray historically overlooked voices, most notoriously in Florida. Why is power threatened by books?

HD: I think I've come to a tentative answer throughout the process of writing *Trust* and talking about it and explaining the book to myself, which is that power and capital can't stand on their own. They cannot subsist by sheer force, by sheer force of political power in the form of violence, for example, or by sheer force of economic power, which can also be very violent. (It usually is, actually.) Both these forms of power desperately need a narrative. They need to be propped up, legitimized, by stories. It just doesn't work without that element. So I have very little patience for people who relegate fiction to some kind of epiphenomenal manifestation of language—to a merely irrelevant symbolic accessory. Fiction, storytelling, narratives in general are what support, in quite a strict sense, political and financial power.

So I don't think power is oblivious to the importance that books have, because of what I just said and because, ultimately, I think power can be defined, not exclusively, but to some extent, as the ability to leave a dent in history. Power is much more than that, of course. This is just an aspect of it. But this notion of history brings us back again to books and the importance of the printed word and the importance of narratives. So I think there is a very clear connection there, and the desire to control what we read has to do with the desire to control a much, much larger narrative: to try to control the shape of the dent.

## V. "FULLY IN CAMP FICTION"

BLVR: Some people fear writer's block or writing a bad book or one that nobody wants to read, or one that the government will suppress. Is there some version of that for you?

HD: Yeah, of course. It's always scary to be in between books. I'm now starting a new novel, and it looks like a mess. I try to remind myself that that is the process, but when you're in it, you kind of forget that. I write in longhand, so I go and look at my notebooks for previous projects, and they look just as messy. But it's not reassuring, because each time, the feeling is fresh. Those moments are a little frightening. And then, eventually, you find that it's growing and you're kind of accompanying the process that is doing its own thing almost—which is a beautiful feeling.

Of course, the fear to suck is deep-seated, especially if you are concerned with the sentence as a unit, which I very much am. So it's not just that one hopes the book as a whole won't suck. I always feel the book is only as good as its worst sentence. I feel the stakes are super high with each clause for me, because that's the way I write. My fears have more to do with the aesthetic side of things—if it's going to work as a piece of literature, more than if nobody will ever want to read it, and other more commercial, institutional concerns.

BLVR: It's interesting how you can have this whole kind of nebulous idea, but then one thing clicks that actually makes it work. For you, that thing that clicks: Is it finding the narrator? Is it a plot moment? Is it understanding where the end is going to come in?

HD: It's not the ending. I've written books without knowing for a really long time how they would end. Like, I'm halfway into it, and I'm not displeased with what I'm doing, but I don't know how it's going to end. That is a familiar feeling. So that's not it. To me, I think it has to do a little bit with what I was talking about, like four questions or so ago, which is when an emotional texture becomes sharper, when an emotion comes into focus and

it merges with a diegetic drive—the emotion and the story becoming the same gesture.

It's very different for each project. For instance, with *Trust*, what made it all come together—and I had written several thousand words—but what made it all come together was when I knew there was going to be a novel within the novel. I liked that idea. And that the real-life tycoon was going to respond to this novel with his own version of the facts. I also liked that idea. That was something I could work with. But when I discovered that it was going to be this young woman who would write the book for the big man, and the voiceless woman would give the loud man his voice—that's when everything came together. That's also when I realized, Oh, wait, this is a book about things I wasn't aware of. It's essentially a book about voice and the nature of storytelling. But for months and months and months, I didn't know it, and I kept writing. I knew it hadn't coalesced yet, but I didn't know how it was going to coalesce.

BLVR: So obviously you've written two books, you write short stories. Have you ever been interested in venturing into writing in other realms, for the screen or the stage or anything like that?

HD: I've written a few screenplays, only one of which was a serious endeavor for real people who had a real shot at making it. And then, in a very Hollywood kind of way, it collapsed and didn't happen. But it got super close, and I don't dislike that screenplay. I haven't read it in forever, but I'd probably stand by it. That is the only thing. And then I've done a bunch of academic writing, and my first published book was a book about Borges. So that's not fiction. But the short answer is no—I am fully in camp fiction. And everything in my life—all the decisions I'm trying to make now are toward remaining there and trying to do only that. That is truly what I want to do. I want to write fiction.

BLVR: Hobbies? Outside artistic endeavors? Anything like that?

HD: No hobbies, no. ✶

# UNCANNY VALLEY OF THE DOLLS

*From wire coat hangers and soda bottles and torn-up umbrellas,*
*Greer Lankton made figures of uncommon beauty*

*by* **ZEFYR LISOWSKI**

PHOTOGRAPHS COURTESY OF:
*The Greer Lankton Collection, Mattress Factory Museum, Pittsburgh, PA*

## 1.

**M**y favorite photo of the artist Greer Lankton was taken in the bathtub. She is young, just twenty-six, and her blond bob is slightly wet, several strands tucked behind her ears. Her shoulder bones stick out, birdlike, from her bare back; her knees are pressed tightly against her chest. She appears to be beaming, but there's a slight discomfort in her eyes.

In the photo, taken by Eric Kroll in 1984, she's confined to the lower sixth of the picture. The bathtub is full of suds. Around her, occupying the majority of the frame, are seven of the dolls she made. One doll is gender-ambiguous, with sagging breasts and a penis protruding as if from a birth canal; two smaller dolls are perched on a windowsill, with pale, sticklike legs and rosy nipples; a bald-headed, blue-lipsticked figure holds an amber bottle in her lacquered hand; a fat doll has big breasts and a beautiful wide stomach circumscribed by a thick pink ribbon and frilly lace right below the belly button; a partially assembled wire-and-cloth armature hangs on the wall; and in the foreground of the picture, sitting on the tub in front of Greer, is a doll that's bigger than her, with skin the color of undyed plaster and hair like a mass of electrical wires, red eye shadow making two deep Vs underneath her eyes, and between her breasts is etched a bloody cross that drips red onto the corset compressing her ribs.

Greer's creations, like all dolls, are uncanny: they are like us, but not. In his 1913 essay "The Unfortunate Fate of Childhood Dolls," Rainer Maria Rilke writes that a doll cannot be made into a person, or even a thing. Dolls, he notes circularly, are ultimately only dolls, fundamentally strangers to us humans. Greer, who is best known for the dolls she handcrafted from the '70s through the early '90s, found companionship in that strangeness. She fashioned gossamer-thin eyelashes and eyebrows, gently curving fingers with methodically painted lilac and periwinkle tips, expertly coiffed wigs set onto heads just several inches across in diameter. Sometimes they appear to be laughing haughtily, but mainly her dolls look unhappy, leering, starved. Perhaps this is because Greer loved "unusually distressing beauty," bodies outside normative standards of gorgeousness: ones that are too much, too thin, or too thick. She made dolls that look like the bodies she loved. "I think when I'm making [my dolls]," she said, "something from me goes into them."

Unlike her dolls, Greer was conventionally attractive, with pointed, fawn-like features and light radiating from the wide, toothy smile that occasionally broke across her face. While Greer's beauty could be intense (all high cheekbones and exposed ribs), it was a beauty she built herself, with a care that was as present in her own being as it was in her dolls. She came out as trans at just twenty years old, to what was, according to her diaries, a largely unsupportive world, and she found herself in her beauty, built whole theories around it. (She regularly laid around talking about beauty, her lifelong friend and sometimes lover, David Newcomb, told me.) But her work also suggests how being an object of desire conceals something more sinister. Her dolls—and her life—speak to the curdle of misrecognition caused by that beauty. Being beautiful means having access to things that those who are not beautiful are refused: dates, money, attention, institutional and otherwise. But it can also mean not having anything besides beauty itself—and that one is confined to being the muse instead of the artist.

Critics didn't necessarily see that same beauty in her work. Marc Lida, in the New York City paper *The West Side Spirit*, called Greer's exhibits "very disturbing"; Mary Thomas, in the *Pittsburgh Post-Gazette*, dubbed her final exhibition, which was held at the Mattress Factory, "victim art"; Jan Avgikos, in *Artforum*, called her work in the 1995 Whitney Biennial "hideously glamorous." True, Greer's work

PREVIOUS PAGE: *Photo by Greer Lankton, 1980s*

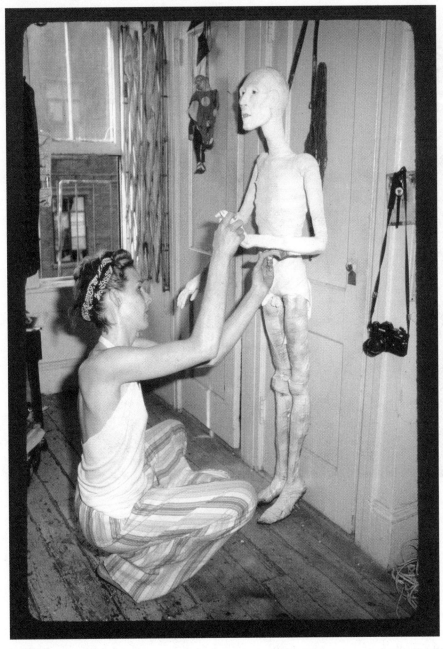

*Photographer unknown, c. 1983*

that fetishizes and hates us simultaneously, is abject, and Greer's dolls are too. They're not gorgeous in the way most women are, but maybe in the way trans women are—a beauty shaped by and against societal expectations. We love ourselves out of necessity when we're around others who don't. Greer explicitly linked her own beauty to her art. "Ever since I was little," she said in a 1984 interview, "I wanted to be a girl. It was an art piece deciding who I was going to be, the process of making myself pretty."

But after she transitioned, Greer rarely referred to herself as a woman in interviews. She identified *as* a woman, she explained, mostly because that was what she looked like. Her dolls, too, resist fixed meanings or identifications; they look *like*, instead of being something essential: their genitals shift regularly, and their faces rearrange themselves and are split and reconstructed and stitched back together from the pieces of one another. As her work suggests, perhaps beauty is a dynamic action, one with the capacity to change. Perhaps beauty is what you do when you're told that you scare others.

I first learned about Greer Lankton through a Facebook message from another trans woman in 2017—four years after I had come out as trans and one year after I had started taking hormones. We'd met in a trans-specific arts scene in New York in which everyone was hooking up with one another, a scene that was notorious among trans people across the country; I had moved from North Carolina to be a part of it. The woman and I had been on several dates, but ultimately settled into a close friendship, trading

unnerves, in that the dolls look almost alive, but not quite. Instead, they exist in a liminal space: the uncanny valley, a term the roboticist Masahiro Mori coined to describe the point at which a robot almost resembles a human. It derives from Freud's concept of the uncanny as a hidden thing that was once familiar, and that has reemerged. To the transphobic viewer, we trans women fall into this gap. Our beauty, constructed against a society

*Photo by Greer Lankton, 1980s*

DMs and texts and sharing drinks with each other. A retrospective of Greer's life and work had opened and closed in 2014, the year before I'd moved to New York, and she sent me an article about it. When she first read about Greer, my friend said in her message, she'd cried. Greer's dolls—stunning, prickly, lovely—mirrored how I felt about my own body: they were alluring and off-putting alike.

Listen: When I first started to transition myself, I was terrified of how rapidly my body was changing: breasts billowing out, body hair vanishing seemingly overnight. So I learned to make myself beautiful to contain the fear, to channel it into presence instead. I comparison-shopped different brands of crimson and coral lipstick, drew my eyebrows on, taught myself to sway from side to side to emphasize my gently swelling hips. And gradually, as I beautified myself (as I was able to beautify myself—beauty, like most things, follows racial and abled lines of power), life became easier. I experienced less street harassment, more employment opportunities. I was quickly learning how I had to look to survive, and I resented that knowledge. Beauty, for me, became simultaneously a shield, a way to dream of a better world, and a violence in what it granted me. In the photo accompanying the article my friend sent, the dolls appeared to struggle with that same burden, hungering under the sharp beam of others' perceptions. *Look at me*, they seemed to demand, their bodies rejecting or meeting those gazes.

"I love this," I messaged her, and I started to cry as well. I had been working so hard at my own beauty that when I first saw the photo of Greer and her dolls in the bathtub, I was startled to see that the dolls rejected the very gaze I had been catering to. Like a light glowing from within, they were beautiful in a way I didn't think possible. It was a beauty I didn't even know I wanted until I saw it, after which there was nothing I wanted more.

## 2.

Greer was born to a Presbyterian family in Flint, Michigan, in 1958. Her father, the minister of the local church, announced her birth by spelling out IT'S A BOY on the church's sign. She was a feminine child, tying a washcloth over her head into pigtails and craving what she later termed "the glamour of a hairdo and lipstick." In a 1996 reflection on her early childhood, she noted, "I never was a flaming faggot... I was atomic." According to Greer, her parents' support often wavered between encouragement and disapproval. Their vexed relationship was only worsened by the profound sense of betrayal she felt about their complicity in the childhood sexual abuse she suffered, from age five onward, at the hands of her maternal grandfather. She failed to receive the protection she deserved.

But nevertheless, Greer endured. She lit up a room with her presence, friends and family said. Throughout her teenage and preteen years, she developed movement and art practices: gymnastics, cheerleading, painting, and doll-making. According to her childhood friend Joyce Randall Senechal, she made her first dolls in middle school, one of which was a life-size teenage boy with long brown hair and a STONED AGAIN T-shirt. He

looked like her at the time: she always wore her hair long. She built the doll out of old sewn-together T-shirts and acrylic paint, and this set a pattern: Greer would construct dolls out of spare materials she found lying around, using wire coat hangers and soda bottles and torn-up umbrellas to make their skeletons, and building out their musculature with clothes she ripped into strips, adding glass eyes to complete the look. "My doll obsession manifest[ed] itself at a very young age," she wrote when she was eighteen. "Dolls became more important than friends.... I feel my dolls in particular are very strong statements about 'the human condition'; by mirroring our exteriors they capture our souls."

Even before her hormonal transition, Greer had been living as a woman. At the 1976 alumni show at the Art Institute of Chicago, which she attended for a year after graduating early from high school, Greer dressed up in a woman suit: a large doll she'd made from cloth and hollowed out, and whom she called Madame Eadie. The doll was voluptuous, without genitalia. In *The Chicago Sun-Times*' review of the show, Greer was misnamed and misgendered, the suit was singled out as the most lurid part of the opening, and Greer's thinness and Eadie's fatness were both emphasized. Greer in the Eadie suit was described as someone "who weighs 120 pounds but dressed up as a grotesque, overweight woman with her belly button hanging out"—the kind of derogatory language that would be used to characterize her work for the rest of her life. In her brief remarks to the *Sun-Times*,

Greer insisted that Eadie was fashionable, not grotesque—which I take as genuine, despite her intense anorexia and hatred of her own body. ("Anything over three digits is a danger zone," she once painted on her bathroom scale.) The journalist, however, viewed her remarks as merely a "claim."

In addition to her remarks, Greer's movements in the suit showed how positively she felt about it. She continued wearing it at college at Pratt Institute, where—at times—she was shy, awkward, and withdrawn. But "when Greer wore Madame Eadie," her Pratt friend Karen Karuza told me, "she was the most confident and magnetic person in the room." There exists little public reflection from Greer on why she made her dolls, but perhaps they became a way for her to model a life before she lived it, a twinning that would continue through her career. Eadie's confidence—like that of Divine, one of Greer's idols—was aspirational for the woman she would become.

At nineteen, after being assaulted at a bar, Greer had a mental breakdown, tried to kill herself, and checked herself into Riverside Hospital in Kankakee, Illinois. She was institutionalized for over two months—the first of several similar incidents in her life. According to case notes, the providers at Riverside often focused on medicating and pathologizing her, rather than on exploring why she was depressed. Later, Greer maintained that they placed too much emphasis on her transness. Treatment notes from the following year describe a person with "strong feminine interests," but in later interviews, she characterized this period as filled with awkward feelings more than with explicit dysphoria. "I was never a man," she said, "just a tortured boy." The hospital forced her sexuality and gender into binaries, telling her she had to choose between being gay and being a woman: she could not be both. Following her hospitalization and a brief period of "trying to be macho," as Joyce Randall Senechal described it, Greer went on hormones.

Two years after her hospitalization, she went to see a surgeon in Youngstown, Ohio, for her vaginoplasty; owing to the flurry of mental health diagnoses she had received during and after her psych-ward stay, she was rejected by several other doctors. She had crowdfunded her surgery through her father's church—in a moment of support for her transition—and ultimately used the money to pay out of pocket for a less reputable surgeon who operated on the side, without medical oversight. Retrospectively, she expressed ambivalence about the surgery. She had felt rushed by both her parents and the medical establishment, and this pressure had resulted in a subpar job. In a 1984 interview, Greer called this doctor's practice "the K-Mart of sex change operations."

After her surgery, Greer's career took off. By the time she was twenty-five, she had appeared in a group show at the MoMA PS1, and had had her first solo show at her friend Dean Savard's gallery, Civilian Warfare, in New York's East Village. "She pursues a deeper intimacy with human anguish and its multiform disguises than many older artists ever dare to deal with, or experience," the novelist

and critic Gary Indiana wrote of the show. He went on to detail the dolls on display: a blood-drenched woman with a semi-erect penis birthing a group of "pepper-shaped" babies attached to a zippered egg sac (*Hermaphrodite*); a flat-chested, broad-shouldered gymnast bending backward to reveal her vagina, staring between her legs with blackened eyes at the viewer (*Pussy Backbend*); a dark-haired boy in an athletic outfit with an erection springing out of his shorts into his hand (*Boy*). In the preoccupations of the show—childbirth, acrobatics, sexuality, the abject, despair—we see the preoccupations of Greer's work and life.

That attention ebbed and flowed throughout her life. By the late '80s, she was in the throes of a turbulent marriage to Paul Monroe, a dressmaker and jeweler, and her work—which she displayed publicly in the windows of his East Village boutique, Einsteins—had seemingly fallen out of favor. She divorced Monroe shortly after he allegedly tried to kill her. (Today, Monroe has an Instagram feed dedicated to Greer's memory.) Trying to detox, Greer moved to Chicago in 1991. There, she distanced herself from many of the people in her life—although she did gain new friends, like Chicago club kid and her apprentice dollmaker Jojo Baby. She received some renewed attention in her last two years, with invitations to be a part of the Whitney and Venice Biennials, and during her retrospective at the Mattress Factory, but after that show, Greer was dead. The papers that had ignored her during her life wrote glowing obituaries.

In an interview with *i-D* magazine in 1985, before she left New York, Greer was asked if her dolls "have problems." "Yes," she said. "Eating disorders, depression, they can't get jobs, their apartment's too small… all the normal problems all of us have. They stay up too late, smoke too much." It would be easy to read Greer's own troubles—drug addiction, romantic unfulfillment, alleged abuse by her intimate partner and family, and above all loneliness—as shaping the work she made. After all, she literally put herself into her art. In an interview, Jojo Baby said that when Greer sewed, she'd accidentally cut her fingers, bleed inside the dolls.

But trans women's art is reduced to autobiography each day. Invariably, everything we make is viewed through the lens of memoir, as opposed to something wholly original. And while Greer's work was admittedly an expression of herself, it was also more than that. She had a life outside of her dolls, and her dolls existed apart from her. Reading her works through the narrow keyhole of her pain eschews their complexity, the multitudes of moods, feelings, and characteristics they both contain and evoke: they're mischievous, scary, and seductive in equal measure. It's tempting to say that Greer's work was her life, but that's also too simplistic. She lived beyond her work; her life was filled with the complexities of being an artist, yes, but also an individual and a trans woman. To remember her solely as a tragic figure—and her work as yoked exclusively to her suffering—does a disservice to her actual life.

## 3.

I suspect that many other trans women have experienced awakenings similar to the one I had in response to Greer's work. I suspect this because so many other trans writers have written about her. There has been a renaissance in pieces about Greer over the past several years, following the digitization of her archives and the publication of her 1977 sketchbook, which she worked on during the year she decided to hormonally transition. Most recent reviews and essays have been by trans women, and most, in turn, contextualize her within a larger ecosphere of trans women. Greer, the reviews emphasize, was like us: a sister lost to time.

This focus on Greer in terms of her connection to a trans community makes sense. Most of the cultural production about her prior to the past several years—obituaries and several pieces in *The New Yorker* and *Artnet* following her 2014 New York retrospective, the very exhibit my friend pointed me to in her initial Facebook message—framed her as an artist existing by herself, absent of any community.

But Greer, as both an artist and a person, didn't stand alone, nor did she have a simplistically supportive relationship with other trans women, as some current writing about her suggests. In interview after interview, she demarcates firm boundaries between herself and other trans women. But she also occasionally let them into her life. It was complicated. "I always love to meet transsexuals," she said, "but few are friends." Yet the relationships she did have are essential

*Photo by Greer Lankton, c. 1985*

to understanding her life and work; the ambivalence she felt toward herself and others prevails.

In a 1992 letter to her friend Jan, Greer mentioned one woman, Regan, whom she'd known for around fifteen years. Greer wrote at length about how much Regan meant to her: As "a transsexual recovering from heroin + cocaine," Regan had a lot in common with Greer, and for a time, the two were

even lovers. "I love her so much," Greer said. Regan was dying of AIDS then, and Greer believed there was nothing she could do to alleviate her friend's pain. She felt she had failed both her friend and herself. In the same letter, she noted, "My parents are very proud of how far I've come, but I feel like I'm just surviving. Not that I don't have BRIGHT moments but it's hard and I'm lonely." Her complex relationship with Regan parallels her relationship with her dolls.

There were other trans women that Greer shared space with—notably the model Teri Toye, whom she tried to pursue a friendship with in the '80s, when they were both in New York. She was rebuffed. Toye reportedly thought that people would gawk if they saw the two of them together, telling Greer, "That's what they *want*." Greer was crestfallen. But despite, or perhaps because of, these relationships, Greer rarely was asked by interviewers about other trans women. She continued to occasionally hook up with trans femmes, and exchanged letters with several, but those relationships were typically complicated. "I feel so much less of a woman with a woman," she once said. Because so few interviewers ever asked about these relationships, it's difficult to ascertain the full extent of her feelings. Regardless, perhaps picking up on her—or society's—reticence to talk publicly, cisgender friends hesitated to associate her too closely with women like her. Greer's former roommate and friend Nan Goldin alluded to this in her request to use her portrait in her 1993 book, *The Other Side*. She wrote: "I'll only include you if you agree to it—I don't know how you'll feel to be in a book where the primary context is transsexuality + drag." It's worth noting, though, that Greer said yes to Goldin's request.

This ambivalence about transness and her trans peers runs through her non-doll work too. In her 1981 watercolor illustration *Coming Out of Surgery*, Greer dramatizes her vaginoplasty. It's a simple painting, moving yet almost cartoonish, the background flush with oceanic blues and mossy greens deep as a forest. Slashed across the frame is a pale body, with pointy angles and sharp Egon Schiele breasts—presumably Greer's. Covering the belly button and forming a panty line is a series of medical-grade bandages, wrapped tightly, dappled pink with blood around the crotch. Through a hole in the bandages, a catheter emerges, bright yellow urine running through it.

But it's the text laid over the painting that's most striking: written in pencil above and below her body are what appear to be memories of the surgery. "She feels a new fullness between her legs which seems to continue into her lower abdomen," Greer writes. "She aches without actually feeling." The text and painting are both immensely tender, gesturing toward pain and becoming simultaneously. It's unclear if the fullness she feels is good or not, which is part of the image's power. It doesn't assign a negative or positive value judgment. It just describes, as if in a state of light dissociation, the aftereffects of her surgery. The work presents transness without endorsement: a transness that's inseparable from the art itself, a transness that reflects her relationship with other trans people too.

I think about this watercolor when I see a later photograph of Greer, also in a hospital bed. Based on how soft her face is, I think she's probably in her mid-twenties, when she had surgery to deepen her navel. Her hospital gown is rolled up to reveal bandages around her stomach. It's a doubled photograph, two pictures collaged on top of each other: a smaller Greer reclining on a larger Greer, her duplicated leg warmers touching. (I see this as a gesture toward complicated community: On the one hand, there's not one trans woman in the hospital bed with her, but two. On the other, they're the same person.) She's smoking in the photos, looking off to the side. On the larger Greer's face, we see the beginnings of a smile. A small brown bloodstain peeks out from beneath the folds at the bottom corner of her hospital gown. The stain would have been right around her midriff, but because the gown is pulled all the way up, it hovers instead right by her heart.

Greer sought medical treatment frequently: in psych wards, in rehabs, and above all in hospitals. Being trans and being sick were twinned experiences for her. Even before her operation, her hyper-extensive joints often slid out of place, and her intense asthma caused her excruciating pain. As a result, she constructed both her life and her transness in relationship to the care she got. In college, Greer told friends that her hormone injections were allergy shots to help with asthma. Her drug use might also have been an effort to replicate the experience of care—as was her arts practice. According to her ex-husband, she built her dolls in an operating theater of sorts, placing herself in the role of doctor. Perhaps she imagined her dolls feeling as safe as she did when she worked on them. Perhaps her pain was shared by them.

Throughout her life, the doll Greer worked on the most was the most like her. Greer started building Sissy in

1979, while recovering from her vaginoplasty. Standing five foot eight and weighing 110 pounds, she had the same proportions as Greer herself. In some photos, Sissy stares out wearily, cigarette dangling from her lips; in others, her green eyes (the same shade as Greer's) are hooded and outlined in black. Sissy had a full set of teeth, which not all Greer's dolls did, and great scooped-out cheekbones and a pronounced jaw. She made her public debut in 1982—fully naked and covered in jewelry, in the window of Einsteins. Greer placed a hand-lettered sign on a tray next to her that said INTRODUCING—SISSY—YOU'RE WELCOME.

Sissy was a constant presence in Greer's life; she worked on and rebuilt the doll up until her death. I'd like to think this was a gesture against loneliness, that Sissy served as a form of community to Greer. But also, in some ways, Greer's relationship with Sissy was fraught. She ripped her dolls open again and again to re-form them, arguably its own kind of violence. And though she worked on her dolls while others were in the room with her, they seem to reflect the isolation she felt elsewhere in her life.

"Symbols always stand alone," the trans woman writer Kai Cheng Thom has noted about her own relationship with community. During her life and posthumously, Greer has largely been perceived as a symbol—as a source of aspiration for trans women and as a tragic loner for others. But when she is, Greer's relationships to both dolls and trans women are glossed over. Our lives, if we long for success or fame—and of course trans women do; being

famous is one of the deepest dreams of those for whom every safety net has been taken away—can silo us away from others like us. Greer's work speaks to the loneliness, violence, and isolation inherent in her pursuit of fame, while pointing to the messy, at times disappointing bonds she formed with other trans women too.

Before she died, Greer reportedly stripped Sissy to reskin her, changing the doll from her likeness to a lover's—perhaps another trans woman. As she disassembled the doll, the blank face underneath the face emerged, then its spindly skeleton. And the doll remained like that for a long time. She didn't get to reassemble the doll before she died, and it hung on a coat hook in the closet of her parents' house for years. Where the heart should have been, she had painted in red ink the same phrase that went inside each of her dolls, clear as the brown on her hospital gown, or the pink between her legs in *Coming Out of Surgery*, or the neatly inked lines in her letter about Regan.

"Love me," it said.

### 4.

Greer died at home on November 18, 1996. She was alone, without her family or friends. She had just completed a retrospective for the Mattress Factory, for which her apartment had been replicated in the museum to be preserved. Per the toxicology report, Greer died of a cocaine overdose; she had started using again to meet the deadlines of her last few shows. According to a letter they wrote to notify friends and family of her death, her parents, who found the

body, weren't surprised. In their letter, they memorialized their daughter's life, using language that was caring, honest, and dismissive.

"Our daughter led a parallel life. She had a bright, creative side… She also had a dark, destructive side (including drugs, an attraction to the 'underside' of society, & abuse of her body). From the first year of life, Lynn [Greer's mother] thought her journey through life would be 'different.' She was born a boy but at 21 she had an operation and became a woman. This never completely healed her difficulties… We supported her emotionally and financially right to the very end."

Crossed out in the middle of the typewritten paragraph in which they described her life were the words "Things could not have gone better."

While Greer's death was ruled an accidental overdose, her illness and previous history of suicidality cast a long shadow over whatever happened. As a child, Greer had checked herself into Riverside because of these impulses, which were also almost certainly related to her sexual trauma. She had attempted to take her own life multiple times: there was one intentional overdose and several accidental ones, in addition to many hospitalizations, both voluntary and involuntary. The fact that Greer was so frequently suicidal is an indictment of the world she lived in—her "difficulties" were not innate, but imposed upon her. But the fact that Greer continued to survive after her first attempt is a testimony to her endurance in the face of hardship nonetheless.

Greer taught Jojo Baby how to make dolls; long after Greer's death, Jojo

*Photo by Baird Jones, 1986*

said they could still hear Greer's voice as they worked. Again and again, throughout my interviews, loved ones emphasized how funny Greer was, how much they'd loved talking with her. "She'd hold court," Karen Karuza said. For those who survived her, these remembered conversations are just as important to their memory as her art is. "Her work was her form of communication," Nan Goldin said in an article on Greer for *The New York Times*, but if it was, it's a one-sided communication: The dolls can't listen or respond to their audience. Only Greer could do that. Her legacy can never fully encompass who she was.

"I am haunted," Kai Cheng Thom writes. "All trans women are. Behind me stretches a line of ghosts—trans women, killed before their time by the hatred of a society that does not know how to love us.… Perhaps this is why trans women dream so deeply—because we walk hand in hand with

those in the next world." No one was with Greer when she died, so it's impossible to know if her death was a suicide or an accident or the result of overwork and neglect. However, the distinctions between those categories (I believe) are blurrier than most would maintain: all point back to the systems that kept her ill. Regardless of what happened, her art reflects a trans woman who tried several times to die but made beautiful things anyway, who had an unfillable emptiness that she tried to fill nonetheless. Her art has lasted because it walks in that next world too.

If you're looking for it, suicide is everywhere in Greer's work. Sissy hanging in the closet. Various dolls' emaciated frames morphing into omens of death. According to her notes for graduate school applications in the mid-1980s, the seven-foot doll posing in her bathtub with a cross carved into her chest was a reference to suicide.

A relative of Greer's had attempted to kill herself in the exact same way years earlier.

*Dolls* is also a slang word for trans women, an irony present in the many profiles written about Greer that compared her to her creations. True, she depicted herself in doll-like poses in pictures throughout her career—including in an ad for her Civilian Warfare show, in which she stretched out fully naked, surrounded by her dolls—but more than that, Greer was a doll herself: a doll who made dolls, a doll surrounded by dolls, alive or not.

Depicting death can also be a way of accessing life, though I don't know if Greer believed that. I know that when I was most suicidal, I dreamed of making a flip-book cataloging every single way I could die: wrists slit, head gored open, body pancaked by jumping off a tall building. By putting it all down, I thought, I could get those urges out of me, could choose life instead of its absence. But I was too scared to actually commit to the project. Drawing these deaths, I feared, would make them more real. Greer's dolls, in contrast to my imaginary sketchbook, are real, and live on after her death—but even they, with their pale skin and bony limbs, look kind of dead anyway.

I can't speak to her motives or thoughts, although I know for myself that when my own suicidality was at its most intense, it was driven by an unalterable sense of loneliness, a sense that my own existence was a punishment, a mistake. I harbored a bitterness that felt inescapable, and that I know, from so many late-night phone calls, other trans women possess as well: feeling as though the world has foreclosed on your life—because in many ways, it has.

It's perhaps hackneyed to say this, but what saved me was the love of others like myself, and the act of embracing the messiness and care present in our lives and work. This complex negotiation echoes what I see in Greer. I, too, have struggled to live. I, too, have struggled to love myself and other trans people. I, too, have realized that loving yourself isn't a panacea for a world that doesn't love you. At various times, I've felt an urgency to live and a simultaneous urge to die. Those same tensions are in Greer's work. I finally realized I've been drawn to her work for all these years because in it I see myself as well.

### 5.

When she was in treatment for drug abuse in the 1990s, Greer made a list of her strengths, jotting them down in red Sharpie. There are twenty-eight items, ranging from "compassionate" to "survivor" to "street smart" to "risk-taker" and everything in between. "Love to learn," one of them says. And toward the end of the list is an entry that is partially scratched out, as if she wanted to say something, stopped herself, and then said it anyway: "wants to be healthy."

By the end of her life, Greer was deep in the throes of addiction, incessantly calling friends to ask for money, and gradually they stopped seeing her because of this. But in her diaries and photos, she described moments of pleasure, however brief. Notes on a night out on the town, a picture of

her beaming next to another trans woman at the Whitney Biennial, a small heart drawn next to the name of a man she'd just had sex with— all are evidence of the happiness and companionship she felt with others. "I will not die," she wrote in her 1977 journal, shortly before deciding to transition. "I will become." On the following page is a drawing of her own face in profile, with garish eye shadow and a sneer. In the drawing, she looks tough and fierce, and she looks beautiful.

All told, Greer made at least three hundred dolls—not including the dolls she remade. Her work is now scattered among various individuals and institutions: private collectors, her ex-husband, David Newcomb, MoMA, and the Mattress Factory, among others. And in this collection—photographs, dolls, journals, and other documentation—her life remains. Greer posing next to a doll, her face heavily lined and crumpled at thirty-six. Greer ten years earlier, staring down the camera over a smoldering cigarette. Greer at twenty, in her freshman year at Pratt, laughing at a joke told by her dorm-mate who snapped the photo. Greer's face sparks with joy, at least for a moment.

"Greer's work was like surgery without anesthesia," Nan Goldin wrote in a *New York Times* remembrance. "Her work came out of her need to create art to survive, and it took tremendous courage to reveal herself to such an extent." But survival wasn't only in her art; it was at the root of her life.

When Greer was fourteen, she had a tooth extracted, and she drew a comic

about it afterward. The drawing, done in pencil, is far more lighthearted than the work she would become famous for, but even then, melancholy still coursed through it. It depicts a bizarre birthing scene, in which a line of "old teeth" is nestled, mostly smiling, into a set of gums. One tooth, blackened with cavities and wearing an expression of resignation, is being yanked out with pliers. "Old tooth being taken up to the big heavenly denture in the sky," reads the caption.

At the bottom of the image is a small human, "a little man in the mouth whose job is to push the new teeth forward to a new life." With arms outstretched, he pushes a baby tooth out through the gumline. The teeth are smiling because they're excited for someone new to arrive. "Welcome," the tooth with the biggest smile says. In the drawing, we see glimpses of a theme that will pervade her work for the rest of her life: a world where vulnerable things are safe, where they endure. Birth is welcomed, and death doesn't hurt. I really hope Greer believed this. I hope every one of us dolls continues living.

When I first saw the picture of Greer Lankton in the bathtub seven years ago, I thought her smile was one of pride in her work: *Look at what I've made!* Now I wonder if it was just a way of saying: *I'm still here. Don't forget me.* In that photograph and others, surrounded by the things she made, she remains: blond hair swept up behind her ears, like she usually wore it, grinning wide with all her teeth in the flash of the camera, looking for all the world like someone who is still alive. ★

# OBJECT

## GLASS TILE

*by Benjamin Cohen*

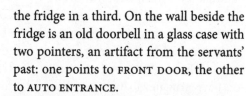

**FEATURES:**

✶ Multicolored

✶ Purchased at the art store in town

✶ Healing

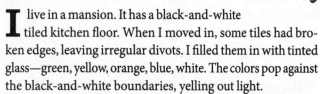

I live in a mansion. It has a black-and-white tiled kitchen floor. When I moved in, some tiles had broken edges, leaving irregular divots. I filled them in with tinted glass—green, yellow, orange, blue, white. The colors pop against the black-and-white boundaries, yelling out light.

It isn't mine, the mansion. I'm the resident faculty adviser for an off-campus house that my college owns. It was built in the 1880s; the college bought it in 1960. About twenty students live here on the second and third floors. My apartment is on one side of the first floor.

I've been upstairs only a few times. The first time was about a month after I moved in. That was after the separation. The prior adviser unexpectedly moved out, leaving the space in want of new occupation. Being broken left me in want of new occupation.

The first time I went upstairs was during a storm, because the power was out. The students were playing cards by iPhone-light. They asked me to join them. I was up there a second time after everyone moved out in the summer, and a friend and I were mutually curious about what the place looked like. It looked really nice, with nooks, small alcoves, study spots, side rooms. It blows my mind that this Victorian Gothic masterpiece is essentially a dorm.

Back in my apartment, the kitchen floor staring at me was less majestic. It reflected back the fractures of a twenty-six-year marriage's end. It was hard to think about; it's hard to talk about. The cracks in the tiles didn't help.

It's somewhat obvious that the apartment was the servants' quarters a hundred years ago. The butler's pantry gives it away. It's about ten by twelve feet, ringed by ten glass-doored cabinets, each with four shelves. I'm currently using three and a half of the forty shelves.

The kitchen is fifteen by fifteen feet, with a mid-century ceramic sink basin in one corner, a stove in another, and the fridge in a third. On the wall beside the fridge is an old doorbell in a glass case with two pointers, an artifact from the servants' past: one points to FRONT DOOR, the other to AUTO ENTRANCE.

The tiles on the floor are distressed, worn and soft. They look like faux limestone, or vinyl marble. I'd date them to the 1950s, like the sink.

There were a few broken tile corners and edges, leaving some gaps and spaces.

I got it in mind to find stained glass, or pieces of glass, or broken colored tiles. I went to an art store in town and asked, "Do you have broken tiles or mosaic pieces or pieces of glass or I'm not sure what? Something colored and various?" A horn-rimmed-glasses clerk stared me down. "No, no, we wouldn't have anything like that." Then he walked back a few aisles to show me something he thought might be close, which was a container of 100 percent exactly what I had been looking for. Either I'm a terrible describer or he was a terrible listener or we maybe met in the middle.

I have a faint memory of seeing an article about mending cracks with misshapen mosaic tiles. Guerrilla street artists used potholes and damaged sidewalks as open canvases to be filled in. They replaced something empty and faded with something living and recovered. I came home and dumped out the small box of broken colored pieces of glass onto the floor, sat down on my knees, and arranged them in the empty spaces. I glued each underside with a silicone epoxy I got at Ace Hardware.

The first space I worked on was the entry to the kitchen. It is a random assortment of different colors. For the next, on the other side, I tried to make it look like a landscape, like a cloud hovering over green reeds and blue water. Except I spaced out, and the clouds (white glass) are in the middle. Which looks just as good.

I needed repair. It's been exhausting, with so much broken. The colors contrast haphazardly with the black and white. Small healing shocks of color stand out against dull chromatic squares. Recovery is a kind of improvement; repair is a kind of solace. ✶

*Illustration by Rich Tommaso*

# MONICA PADMAN

[PODCASTER]

"IT'S FINE IF PEOPLE DON'T THINK
I'M KNOWLEDGEABLE ABOUT EVERYTHING. I'M NOT.
AND, BY THE WAY, NOBODY IS."

Jobs Monica Padman had with Dax Shepard and Kristen Bell
before starting *Armchair Expert* with Dax Shepard:
*Nanny*
*Personal assistant*
*Listicle ghostwriter*

To interview Monica Padman is to interview an interviewer. Padman is the cohost of the astronomically popular podcast Armchair Expert, *cohosted by actor Dax Shepard, of the television shows* Parenthood *and* Punk'd. *In 2019,* Forbes *listed* Armchair Expert *second on its inaugural list of top-earning podcasts; in 2020,* Forbes *estimated its monthly audience to be twenty million listeners. In 2021, Padman and Shepard signed a deal with Spotify that was rumored to be eight figures. Their guests have ranged from public figures (Barack Obama, Monica Lewinsky) to Hollywood stars (Gwyneth Paltrow, Kerry Washington) to "experts" (Ronan Farrow, Atul Gawande), to Shepard's mom, in a refreshingly surprising mix, all guided by Shepard's wide-ranging intellectual interests. Since the show premiered, in February 2018, the team has released over five hundred episodes. Now, in addition to* Armchair Expert, *Padman and Shepard produce eleven shows under their "Armchair Umbrella."*

*Illustration by Kristian Hammerstad*

*When I first learned about* Armchair Expert, *the concept did not appeal to me. A celebrity talking to other celebrities? I'd been listening to hyperproduced podcasts like* This American Life *and* Serial, *and conversational podcasts like the madcap* Mike and Tom Eat Snacks *or Marc Maron's* WTF. *What I loved about those shows was their specificity. Their hosts weren't massively famous, and that resulted in more interesting conversations. Celebrities spoke through the neutered filter of PR, or so I thought. But* Armchair Expert *surprised me. Shepard and Padman's guests—celebrity or otherwise—were strangely willing to just… speak. They were vulnerable, and compelling in their vulnerability. Often these conversations were a far cry from other, more carefully polished interviews. The cohost combination was unique: as an actor, Shepard could draw guests from his rarefied world. But Padman interested me too. She didn't speak much during the conversations between Shepard and the guests. But her voice was heard prominently on every episode's "fact-check," when she verified details that had been stated on the show. The fact-checks were not particularly rigorous: she did not adjudicate every fact. Instead, the segments were an opportunity for Padman and Shepard to catch up on each other's lives, with equal parts vulnerability and transparency—to an audience of millions.*

*It's a formula that has, of course, won them many devoted listeners. But it's also led to detractors. Online, there is no shortage of criticism and judgment of both Padman and Shepard, especially since their immense success.*

*I'm guilty of harboring my own judgments. Padman is an Indian American woman in a white-dominated space who has spoken openly about her struggles with self-esteem and self-acceptance. I have wished for a different arc for her: a liberation from—and rejection of—Western beauty standards, a promotion from sidekick status. But in speaking with her, it occurred to me that my thinking was its own racist catch-22: wanting someone in the spotlight to represent the universal person-of-color experience, which doesn't actually exist. Padman reminded me that we often bring preconceived notions to our encounters. But we need to shed those assumptions in order to fully be present with another person, in order to listen exactly to what they are saying.*

*I am a novelist, and in that medium, there is the opportunity to revise and revise again. Appearing as a guest on podcasts has never come naturally to me; in fact, it's frightened*

*me. With verbal communication, there is an ingrained imperfection, an inability to fix one's mistakes. But speaking with Padman, I was struck that imperfection could be a feature—instead of a bug—and could lead to greater intimacy and connection. Making mistakes in conversation: it's human, and it's what we have in common.*

*The interview was pushed several times because of Padman's busy recording schedule. We met at one of her favorite spots, a neighborhood restaurant in Los Feliz, Los Angeles. She already felt familiar: I had heard so many hours of her speaking. The first thing I asked was if she was nervous about being the interviewee instead of the interviewer. "It's always a little nerve-racking to not know what you're entering," she told me. "But it's also fun. Somewhere in between."*

—*Rachel Khong*

## I. STICKING WITH IT

THE BELIEVER: So you came to Los Angeles for acting.

MONICA PADMAN: It's funny, because the reason I pivoted into this other realm is because I could not get work as an actor. Now, since I've been podcasting, more opportunities have come up within acting, but I have to turn a lot of those down because priorities have shifted. The idea that I would turn down an audition… it was impossible. That would never, ever have happened. But here we are.

When I came out here, I didn't have an agent or anything. I'd send my headshot and résumé. On IMDb, I'd search all the managers and agents and send my stuff out. Brutal, just brutal. I was babysitting to get by. Then an assistant at Odenkirk Provissiero responded and said, "Hey, you're a little green, but keep in touch with me." So I did. I just kept sending her things like *I'm at Upright Citizens Brigade [UCB]. Now I'm doing this. I did this.* She started sending me on auditions, and then I started booking small things here and there. But it was hard. It's exactly what you know it to be—full of rejection. I did have a really, really lucky streak in commercials, which was such a lifesaver. It was fun and paid well. And, of course, once I started nannying for Kristen [Bell] and Dax [Shepard], I started working a lot more in commercials and as an actor, because the desperation had faded. I had this other stable thing. That's such a common piece of advice for actors: *Leave the desperation at the door. Go in as if you don't need it, and have fun.* And you can't. It's so much easier said than done. The only way you can do it is by having an actual sense of safety in other parts of your life.

BLVR: What were you doing between auditions?

MP: Babysitting. I had multiple families I was juggling. And writing spec scripts. I also started doing improv with UCB. I took tons of classes, and I was on multiple teams, multiple practices a week. I was just trying to fill the day and stay busy. I would go on daily walks with one of my other actor friends, for an hour around the neighborhood. It's a real struggle to keep your head above water. But I had heard early on—and this was such good advice—to have other eggs in your basket, to fill out the rest of your life and not be so singularly focused on acting. And I really did that. I had a great group of friends. I do look back on that time with such fondness. We bounced around and had fun and dreamt together. It was a very special time.

BLVR: Do you think there's something about you that made you not quit? We've all heard the stories of people giving up.

MP: It's a tale as old as time. That's fully my friendships. That's the only reason. I had a community, and that was the saving grace—not just other actors. My roommate Anthony was a writer—is a writer. At that point, he was a writer's assistant. I have a friend who is our producer and he was a PA. Everyone was at the nascent stage of their journey. And that's so critical. We'd pick up more and more friends along the way. I don't think I would be here if I hadn't had that. It was just too demoralizing. Unless you have someone to come home to, and commiserate with.

## II. "I'LL DO THAT"

BLVR: How did you go from being a nanny for Dax and Kristen to cohosting a podcast?

MP: At first it was date-night babysitting. Lincoln would probably have been six or seven months old. I mean, the first handful of times I didn't even see her. I got there, they had put her down, and they were out to a date night. And I would just watch TV and do my nails. Kristen would say, "I have this gel nail kit if you want to use it." And I'd think,

What is this place? It's so amazing. When Delta was born, they asked if I could come on full-time. I said yes.

I would come every morning. And it was really all hands on deck, whoever was there. Kristen was in and out; Dax was in and out. He was working on *Chips* at the time, and Kristen is one of the busiest people I've ever met. You would just look around and see what was needed, whether it was doing laundry for the baby or dishes or taking Delta on a walk or to the swings. It was a village mentality. Which was nice because it didn't feel stressful. It wasn't like *You have to do this and then this*—it was very loose.

I would be there all day. And at night, sometimes I would go home, but sometimes I wouldn't. Sometimes I would stay and the adults would play games or watch TV—we had so many shows we would watch. And I just became a part of that family. They *let* me be a part of that family. It was really special.

When Delta went to school, they said, "We love you. We really want to keep you here. But obviously we don't need a nanny every day while she's at school. We're just letting you know where our heads are at." And I got so anxious: I'm going to have to leave this job, but I love it. I love this place and these people. I thought, Oh my god, that's it. How sad. And then Kristen asked, "Would you want to transition to an assistant role—for me?" And I said, "Sure, great. I'll do whatever." And she hadn't had one at that point, so I got to create that role.

Her publicist would send things: *Hey, do you want to do this article, ten things you love about blah, blah, blah?* And I would receive the emails as her assistant. And at one point, I thought, Oh, she's so busy, she won't be able to do this. Maybe I could do it. Then I just asked her, "Do you want me to write this?" And she said, "Is that something you do?" And I was like, "Yeah, I do. I write." I just started taking on more and more and more. So we became creative partners, me and her, even before the podcast stuff happened.

And at one point Dax said, "I want to do a podcast!" He was just saying it. And I said, "I could probably figure out how to do that." So I started reaching out to people I knew who had podcasts, just poking around. Then he was like, "I think you should be on it." And then we started it.

BLVR: What did you know about podcasting at the time?

MP: It was still the early days, of course, compared to now. But there were still a lot of them back then. The joke was that at first Dax said, "I think we should call it *The Millionth Podcast.*" But it still felt sort of niche. *Totally Laime* was a podcast I loved. It's a couple and they interview comedians. And they had another show where they just talked, and another show, after they had kids, about motherhood. I reached out to Elizabeth Laime, one of the hosts of that show, and I was like, "Can I talk to you?"

And she said sure. I just asked her all the questions, like "Technically, how does it work? And what do you think makes a good one?" At that point, I realized I didn't necessarily want to do the soundboard. So we brought in Rob [Holysz]. Dax had done a few podcasts as a guest. And that's why he wanted to do it. He really loved the long-form conversation. But we had no idea what we were doing. We had Kristen on as the first guest. And I didn't talk at all; I just sat there. We were figuring out what we were doing. Dax was admittedly very controlling.

But it was fun. We thought, Let's do it again. It took a while for us to find our footing. But for better or worse, we put all those episodes out, whether they were ready to go or not. A few episodes in, we decided to start editing. And I was like, "OK, I'll do that."

### III. VULNERABILTY

BLVR: People often talk about how comfortable they feel on the podcast, and how open you both are. How do you approach interviewing? And how do you sort of set the stage for this intimate, vulnerable space?

MP: Dax and I are doing different things. He is a master at making people feel comfortable, in life in general. I do sometimes try to remember when I first met him. He can have an intimidating presence. He's a big dude. A very smart one. And a very funny one, and a gregarious one. So that can be a little intimidating. But he asks a lot of questions, and cares to know. It doesn't seem obligatory. That's a superpower of his. And he brings that to the room. He also leads with all his own issues and vulnerabilities and insecurities. It's pretty hard, when someone is doing

that, to keep your door fully closed. I think because he leads with vulnerability, people just follow. I said really early on, "Oh god, I don't know if I want to be so open about all this stuff." And he said, "Well, you don't have to be. But it *is* the compelling part of being human."

I couldn't be more open at this point. After he said that, I had to make that decision. Especially on the fact-checks. On the fact-checks it's just me and him. And we're best friends, so we talk about everything. And I think that was when I first thought, Oh god, we just talked about that. I don't know if I want that out there. And that's when he said, "You can take that out if you want. But I do think these are the things that actually connect us as people." And so I thought, Sure, why not? I had this weird hang-up, though. I was like, "What about when I meet my husband? Is it unfair to him that everyone else gets to know these intimate parts? Like, shouldn't some of it be saved for him?" I had this bizarre idea about that. And Dax said, "There will always be things between you and your husband that don't get shared. The details of life." And so I just fully jumped in. Ever since, I've just been very open. People feel it. It's a very intimate space that I think lends itself to that. There are pictures of us all over the wall. There's a painting of me as a baby. It's a bit disarming. Which lends itself to people just wanting to chat. We say, "You can cut stuff if you want," and that frees people up a lot. We both have the goal of coming in fully open with our own stories.

BLVR: How is it working with someone you're so close to? Where do you draw boundaries, if any? How do you manage all that, having a creative partner who is also a friend?

MP: It's hard. And we've gotten better over time at boundaries. Not only are we such good friends, but I'm in the family in some ways. It's a big old entanglement. And we're both really opinionated people. And we are comfortable with each other. So we have big fights, and we have not-great moments. But we've gotten better about understanding each other's needs, especially in conflict. It's like any relationship.

You understand how to communicate with that person in conflict. We've gotten better about that, and at boundaries in general. When we're here, we're here. This has to be somewhat professional. It's hard because the crux of the show is intimacy and friendship. Talking about, you know, your poop… it's so ridiculous. And then to also say, *But it has to be professional!* is a very weird thing. We don't always hit the mark. But I think we do a pretty good job. And we've gotten better and better—out of respect for each other. We don't want to be fighting. It's not helpful, and it's not fun for us if we're fighting over something with the show. But then we come in to interview and we have to be all smiley. I think the audience can also feel it. We're not that good at hiding it. To our credit, sometimes we'll just say it. We'll just talk about it—"Well, we're in this fight"—or it'll come up. And we'll have it sort of aired out there. But it's complex. I think anytime you work with friends, it's hard. And now I work with Liz [Plank] on *Synced*. It's a similar thing. You have to know when to take the friendship hat on and off. But it's learned over time. I don't think anyone is perfect at it.

### IV. THE JACKPOT

BLVR: Is it satisfying to you to hear the hard stories of people who are really successful?

MP: For sure. I mean, it's the most relatable thing. We can't be at the top of the mountain all the time. And they're not. We as a society do a very strange thing with celebrities, and *to* them. We dehumanize them. In a lot of ways that are good for that celebrity's ego, but then also not. The ability to attack them. Showing that everyone's a real person is important to me, and it gives me a lot of empathy and compassion: *I don't know you. I can think I do, based on what you're presenting. But I don't.* I think it's helpful to remember that.

BLVR: It's interesting to hear you talk about dehumanization and what we think of celebrities. And now you're sort of sucked into this, right? People can be so dehumanizing to hosts of podcasts. I wonder what your experience of this fame has been like. People really feel like they know you, because it's such an intimate form.

MP: They do. And to an extent they do. They know *a lot* about me. I think my relationship to being adjacent to the public

eye has been fairly positive. Because if they listen, and they continue to listen, for the most part they like us, and they like what we're doing, and so when they run into us on the street, they're nice. The issue I find, mainly, is people who don't listen. And who just want to be on social media and comment and have their opinion heard, but haven't heard the show and don't know us. They just want to be loud. I think it's very toxic and a problem. But I do a good job of really recognizing that it's so not about us or me. And also I just don't look at it. I have a rule: I don't look at comments.

BLVR: Was that always in place? Or did you look at them in the beginning?

MP: Pretty early on I saw one I hated. And I thought, This is not good for me. You feel the negative ones ten times more than a positive one. At some point not that long ago, I said, "No, I'm not doing it." Dax was like, "Oh, we need to go through the comments," and I was like, "No. Me and you are not going to do that. We can have somebody else do that for us, but *we* should not be doing it." And I really stand by that. I really don't think it's healthy at all. Especially right now. It's a really toxic space.

BLVR: When you started the show, Dax was already famous. Something we have in common is that I also worked for a very famous man. I was an editor at *Lucky Peach*, which is a food magazine that Dave Chang started. When you're working for someone so famous, you're automatically part of something cool. And you get the credit for the cool stuff, and you *are* doing a lot of work on it, so of course you should get the credit. But I'm just wondering how that was for you, to be working with this really famous man who takes up a lot of space, for better and worse.

MP: I think it was mainly for the better. Because he'd already done it. He already knew what that path looked like. And so this wasn't divergent. For me it was new. So it was kind of nice to have someone who'd already walked the walk. With him and Kristen, having those examples was very helpful. He's also extremely protective. So it's helpful to have someone in your orbit who knows the world, who's protective not only of the business but of me personally. Early on, I was saying to him, "I don't know, I'm just sitting here. I don't think I'm contributing enough. And I feel really insecure when we have these people on who are my idols. And I don't know that there's a place for me to say anything. Who am I? And they're going to think I'm stupid, because I'm just sitting there." And he was like, "I do understand all that. And we can work on that together. But also, I want you to know that we hit the jackpot. And I know—only because I've been doing this for so long—that this does not happen. You maybe get one lottery moment. Most people never get any, and at most you get one or two. And you're in one. So I want you to also be able to feel that and, like, acknowledge and be happy about that. Don't give all your energy to what is not happening instead of to what is happening." And that was really helpful to me, seeing the overall picture of: Oh yeah, we are talking with the most interesting people. And not just talking—listening to their stories. Also, me and him get to shoot the shit all day long as a *job*. We're getting money for it. Who would have ever thought? So it really did put things in perspective. It didn't mean I was like, OK, I'm happy to just be silent now. That wasn't the case. It was like, I need to figure out exactly my lane here, which I do think I did. So his having been in this business for a long time has been very helpful to me.

### V. MAKING YOUR VOICE HEARD

BLVR: How did you make that shift into a role that is more proactive?

MP: One way was truly just logistical. We had Jake Johnson on the show early on. And the way our seats were arranged, Dax sat across from the guest. Every time I would talk, the guest would have to pivot their whole body to address me. And it was uncomfortable. It always felt like I was interrupting. And at one point, Jake Johnson said something like, "I can't see her. Is there any way we can adjust this?" So we brought over a chair and sat in more of a triangle. And from then on we changed the seating arrangement completely. It changed a ton! I no longer felt like I had to be like, *Excuse me. I want to say something now!* I still have to balance when to interrupt the flow and when not to. But it's so much better when the guest can see both our faces. And my confidence has grown. I used to think, Oh my gosh, we have *this* person coming in. It's so exciting. I've seen all their movies. I can still get excited, but I don't feel

I have to prove myself anymore. Which is such a burden off my shoulders, and has led to so many more interesting thoughts from me.

BLVR: How do you think that shift to more confidence happens?

MP: I think it's just time. It's being around so many people I've had on pedestals that I could see were really just people. Also I edit the show. So cleaning up everyone has given me a ton of confidence. Cleaning up Dax, cleaning up myself, cleaning up the guests. Everyone's fallible; we're all making mistakes. And it has given me a lot of control, making these edits. Being the overall decision-maker about what gets put out and what gets cut. That's another piece: I edit the show, I produce, I make a lot of creative decisions. A lot of confidence is produced there.

BLVR: Did you ever feel nervous about having more of your voice heard? Or was it always just something you were comfortable with? Because that's something I've really struggled with: being in the public eye as a writer.

MP: Yes and no. I love deep-diving into any sort of conversation. With friends, with anyone. I'm just so uninterested in surface-level anything, so in some ways this format is definitely up my alley. It's much easier than having a three-minute sound bite—*that* scares me. But this, no, because I can clarify things if I need to. You have the space to *be*. I feel comfortable there. And, again, doing it with my best friend feels easy and natural. It's funny, because we have all these shows at this point, different iterations. We have *Flightless Bird* and *Synced*, and I'm on all these shows. And they're all so fun and wonderful and very special. And they each have their own fingerprint and dynamic, but nothing is going to compare with that original one. It's very—for lack of a better word—celestial. You get lucky sometimes, and that's just the truth. People will ask, "How do you do it?" You can't tell people how to have chemistry. So there's some luck in there for sure.

### VI. TYPES

BLVR: When I listened to you guys for the first time, I just assumed that you were a small, Terry Gross–looking white lady with a pixie cut and glasses.

MP: Oh, that's funny.

BLVR: In part because when you think of podcasts, you think of two white guys talking—at least that's the image I had from podcasts of several years ago. And Dax, he's definitely his own person. But he's also very much this type: He's a knowledgeable man. He's very charming. And as a listener, you know that type immediately. People are just familiar with it. And they know it and are amenable and open to that type. There's less of a model for what you're doing and who you are. I'm wondering how that has been for you. Did you go into it thinking, There aren't any models of what I'm doing on the radio? Or did you already have the confidence to just be who you were?

MP: That's a very interesting question. I haven't thought about that, actually. I definitely didn't have any models. I

---

## WRITINGS THAT WERE LOST AT ONE POINT BUT EVENTUALLY FOUND

✶ "The Fall of Gondolin" by J.R.R. Tolkien
✶ "Temperature" by F. Scott Fitzgerald
✶ *The Original of Laura* by Vladimir Nabokov
✶ "The Doll" by Daphne du Maurier
✶ *Go Set a Watchman* by Harper Lee
✶ *Murder at Full Moon* by John Steinbeck
✶ *We'll See Each Other in August* by Gabriel García Márquez
✶ *The Dark Interval* by Rainer Maria Rilke
✶ "The Incident of the Dog's Ball" by Agatha Christie
✶ *Juneteenth* by Ralph Ellison
✶ *The London Scene* by Virginia Woolf
✶ *Barracoon: The Story of the Last "Black Cargo"* by Zora Neale Hurston
✶ *Hear the Wind Sing* by Haruki Murakami
✶ *Mary Ventura and the Ninth Kingdom* by Sylvia Plath
✶ *The Big Box* by Toni Morrison
✶ *Black Nativity* by Langston Hughes
✶ "Where Is the Voice Coming From?" by Eudora Welty
*—list compiled by Claire Fairtlough*

---

think because of the nature of how this all started… In retrospect, it sounds like we're being humble-braggy. We did not know what it was going to be at all. So I wasn't thinking, Oh gosh, I'm entering this foray and don't have anyone to look to. It was just us doing what we already did in the backyard. Bringing it onto microphones.

I have to give Dax credit for that. He said, "We need your voice here, a voice that's not like mine, that brings something to the table—a background to the table—that I don't have and can't ever have." He is a tall, white, charismatic, muscular alpha male. With a ton of privilege, but because of his upbringing, growing up with a single mom and a lot of trauma, he has a through line of always wanting to be better. If he doesn't understand something, he'll say, "OK, I'm confused about that." He is not so cemented in his beliefs, which is why we can do what we do. I would not be interested in doing this with somebody who was closed off to hearing a different opinion. I'm not interested in that at all. So I do give him a lot of credit for saying, "I think we need another voice here." I do think some people, when they hear us, they're like, "Well, why don't you talk as much as him?" And, first of all, it's a little flattering that people want to hear more. But also, that's not the setup. That's not the show. The show isn't *The View*. It's not me and him equally interviewing. It's him, and that was always the case.

BLVR: I find it so interesting that you are often willing to just not know something. Dax has a lot of convictions. He knows a lot of stuff. And you're just a lot more open about *not* knowing stuff and being OK with that. I think that's something I hadn't really seen before, or heard on the radio. We're so used to experts talking to one another. Was that something you cultivated? Or did it come more naturally for you?

MP: It was natural. I think it's probably more natural for women—again, for better or worse—to enter any conversation saying, *I'm not so sure*. Even when we are sure. So sometimes it can be a detriment. But I would say it's my role there that allows it. If I were in charge of directing the whole interview, I might be less likely to not know, because then where does the interview go? There is some function to having a point of view and directing the conversation. It's easy for me to add in something a little bit more ambiguous. It's nice that we can have both things happening.

BLVR: Not to just tell you criticism after you said you don't look at it, but often the criticism of the show is that you're not speaking up or that you don't seem as knowledgeable. It strikes me as ingrained misogyny. They almost want this masculine-expert energy to be there that doesn't necessarily need to be there, or benefit the show.

MP: We're not doing a book review. We're trying to have a conversation with people about their lives. When we have experts on, of course, it is a little bit of a different thing. And I don't know as much. I often don't read the books. It's by design. It's fine if people don't think I'm knowledgeable about everything. I'm not. And, by the way, nobody is. I'm not going to pretend I am for the benefit of other people. And, again, my role on those episodes is to act as the audience, to fill in gaps. And also to add some flavor, for lack of a better word. It doesn't bother me, because I do know what I'm doing, and I know it's critical to the show, whether they think so or not. If it wasn't there, they would feel it.

BLVR: To me, it seems horrifying to have everything you say be so scrutinized. Especially when it feels very conversational for you in the moment, just talking with a friend.

MP: I just don't look at the comments. If it's not in my orbit, I don't have to feel it. And I just keep it out. Because, I don't know, my life is so privileged and happy and good on a day-to-day basis, and I get to do something I love with people I love. I can't let other people ruin that.

BLVR: Dax has said stuff like *Oh, Monica's here so that I don't say something racist or sexist.* How do you feel about that?

MP: I actually appreciate it. I think it's honest. To say, *There's this person here who keeps me in line.* Because, like you said, on a lot of other shows, they don't

have that. They have people with big egos talking at or to each other without anyone bringing it back. I will say, even just my presence in the room as a minority makes people think differently. It makes people think a little bit more before they speak, and that's great. I want people to practice thinking before they speak. It does take practice if you're a certain kind of person who's grown up never having had to check yourself. You can go through your whole life without ever thinking before you speak, and there are really no repercussions.

BLVR: Did you feel equipped to be that person, or did you think: I also have internalized misogyny or racism?

MP: We talk about that all the time. It's ubiquitous; it's everywhere. It's actually why we can have those types of conversations: because I am not saying I'm perfect at it. No one is. And Dax doesn't feel attacked, because I'm just a person too. But I do feel equipped. I know my experience on earth. And that's all I can share. As a brown kid growing up in Georgia, and being a woman, and all those things. But I also don't think everything's so black-and-white. I'm not trying to put hard lines of us-against-them. I'm there to share my thoughts and opinions based on my experience. Which is a very different experience from his. And his experience is very different from mine. I've learned a ton about addiction that I would never have been exposed to before. It's taught me so much. It's given me so much compassion and understanding. And so I think it goes both ways.

### VII. "FIGURING IT OUT"

BLVR: How do you feel you have grown since doing the podcast? How have you changed as a person?

MP: I think mainly that, since doing this with Dax, I'm much less judgmental. Also, we've never had a person on the show who leaves and we think, They're awful. Even when they come in and we think, This is going to be hard—or, I have preconceived notions about this person. Everyone leaves the show as a real person with multiple dimensions. I might not like everything about them, but I probably like at least one thing about them. And it has helped me so much to see the world in full shades of gray. And I'm grateful for that. When I first started out, I had a lot of opinions about right and wrong, and good and bad, and what you should do or shouldn't do, and now that's all gone. Behind every person there's complexity.

BLVR: I recently listened to the episode when you were hypnotized. I loved what you asked for: to look in the mirror and like what you see. And I wondered if you could talk about that desire.

MP: It's so old. And I think it comes from growing up as a minority in a pretty white state. It's hard because I hated that about myself. I hated that I was different: I was visibly different. That was something I just couldn't change. There was so much self-loathing. And the mirror is the physical image of me. I know it's outdated. I know I've outgrown that, or should have outgrown that by now. But some of these things are just so deep. And the hypnosis was an attempt to get rid of it. I don't know if it worked. I think it maybe helped? Again, my confidence has grown. We said recently on a fact-check that he and I both are going to try to stop that narrative, because we do talk about it a lot, across the board. "Oh, we don't like the way we look." It's kind of boring at this point. And I'm over it. I'm sure people listening are definitely over it. I think I'm done saying that. Which hopefully is also just good for me: to not have that narrative always running.

BLVR: That's something I think about a lot: how boring it is to have the same narrative. The thing that you're constantly playing on repeat, the story you're telling yourself about yourself and how that crowds out the space for more interesting thoughts. I definitely relate to that, and more recently I've realized it's not actually a problem with me. It's a problem with the culture. The indoctrination of Western, American culture saying it's better to be similar to one another than to be different. You've mentioned the confidence of being on the show itself, and how that gave you more empowerment. Do you think you've also learned things through the guests on the show?

MP: Oh my goodness, so many. The true gift is hearing people's stories. Everyone has a nugget of wisdom, whether they know it or not. And it normally comes out at some point in these interviews. I don't know if that really gives confidence so much as context to the world, which is helpful. As we're sitting here and I'm thinking about it a little more, I think if I wasn't doing a lot of the behind-the-scenes stuff, I wouldn't feel very good at that job, necessarily. I might feel excited to be there. But I don't think I would feel secure. I feel good and proud because of what we've built, and what we've built is not the conversations; it's a space that people come to and feel vulnerable in. That's what I'm proud of. And that gives me confidence. We made this. This was nothing and now it's a thing! And that's really emboldening.

BLVR: It sounds very enriching for you personally. Did you feel hesitant to work out some of the things you work out publicly on the podcast—for example, about your struggles growing up Indian American in Georgia? I mentioned that I found it refreshing that you just don't have the answers. You're struggling through these things on the air. Was it a decision to share what you've been through, or did you feel nervous that you were going to say the wrong thing? Because identity stuff can be fraught. I'm working it out privately, but working it out publicly is so exposing.

MP: It is exposing. But I've never felt like, Am I going to say this wrong? Because I can't say the wrong thing about my own life. People can say I'm saying the wrong thing, but they're wrong. I'm talking about me, and me only, and my experience, and hopefully whatever I'm saying helps someone else. Maybe? Or maybe not. Maybe it turns a light on that they weren't thinking about before. Or maybe not. I'm not here to say, *This is how you fix a thing. This is me on the other side of struggle.* We're all struggling every day. And to act like we have answers is a lie. And I don't think that's helpful. That just makes other people feel like, Well, why don't I have the answers? You shouldn't. Because life is about figuring it out today and tomorrow and the next day—evolving. You don't just figure it out and you're done. So I don't think too hard about how it's coming across. Because it's just my story. They can be mad about how I'm telling my story, but they didn't live it. ★

## CURRENT BURN LEVEL

*Tepid at best* ———————— *Third degree*

| A | | |
|---|---|---|
| TERM | FIELD | FIRST USE |
| academese | writing | 1917 |
| acephalous | writing | 1746 |
| advertainment | film & tv | 1999 |
| AI art | visual art | 2018 |
| airport novel | writing | 1972 |
| Apple Store chic | visual art | 2008 |
| arena rock | music | 1977 |

| B | | |
|---|---|---|
| b movie | film & tv | 1948 |
| b side | music | 1949 |
| beach read | writing | 1985 |
| biter | music | c. 1980 |
| bodice-ripper | writing | 1978 |
| brostep | music | 2010 |
| bubblegum pop | music | 1969 |
| butt rock | music | c. 2000 |

| C | | |
|---|---|---|
| cacology | writing | 1775 |
| camp | visual art | 1909 |
| cardboard cutout | film & tv | 1956 |
| cash grab | film & tv | 1987 |
| cheese metal | music | 2000 |
| chick flick | film & tv | 1964 |
| chick lit | writing | 1988 |
| chopsocky | film & tv | 1974 |
| claptrap | writing | 1727 |
| clickbait | writing | 1999 |
| coffee shop art | visual art | 2013 |

| | | |
|---|---|---|
| corporate art | visual art | 1960 |
| corporate Memphis | visual art | 2019 |
| cursive singing | music | 2009 |

| D | | |
|---|---|---|
| dad rock | music | 1994 |
| dauber | visual art | 1655 |
| diatribe | writing | 1581 |
| dime novel | writing | 1860 |
| direct-to-video | film & tv | 1987 |
| doggerel | writing | 1387 |

| E | | |
|---|---|---|
| ear candy | music | 1977 |
| earworm | music | 1978 |
| easy listening | music | 1965 |
| elevator music | music | 1945 |
| exploitation film | film & tv | 1946 |

| F | | |
|---|---|---|
| fan fiction | writing | 1939 |
| fauxtography | visual art | 2006 |
| filler episode | film & tv | c. 1990 |
| flop | film & tv | 1944 |

| G | | |
|---|---|---|
| garreteer | writing | 1653 |
| glurge | writing | 1998 |
| grindhouse | film & tv | 1923 |

| H | | |
|---|---|---|
| Hallmark verse | writing | 1976 |
| hammy | film & tv | 1929 |
| hokum | theater | 1906 |
| hotel art | visual art | 1918 |
| humstrum | music | 1882 |

| I | | |
|---|---|---|
| inspirational art | visual art | c. 2000 |
| instapoetry | writing | 2015 |

*Oldest term with highest current burn*

Coming from a tradition of snobbery likely as ancient as the earliest cave drawing, the derogatory art term has an ample history. When one observes these epithets throughout time, mysterious patterns emerge, old words take on new meanings, and, in many cases, we learn as much about the insulter as we do about the insulted. This schema of art-world snark is intended

# WITHERING ART BURNS

| Term | Category | Year |
|---|---|---|
| int'l art English | writing | 2012 |
| **J** | | |
| jeremiad | writing | 1780 |
| journalese | writing | 1882 |
| jumping the shark | film & tv | 1985 |
| **K** | | |
| kitsch | visual art | 1921 |
| **L** | | |
| l'art pompier | visual art | c. 1900 |
| logorrhea | writing | 1892 |
| **M** | | |
| mall punk | music | 2001 |
| mary sue / gary stu | writing | 1973 |
| mass-market fiction | writing | c. 1950 |
| maundering | writing | 1853 |
| mawkish | visual art | 1702 |
| millennial whoop | music | 2016 |
| mockbuster | film & tv | 2006 |
| mummery | theater | 1549 |
| muzak | music | 1935 |
| **N** | | |
| nostalgia bait | film & tv | 2012 |
| **O** | | |
| oscar bait | film & tv | 1948 |
| overacting | theater | 1611 |
| **P** | | |
| penny dreadful | writing | 1861 |
| pen-pusher | writing | 1899 |
| periergia | writing | 1550 |
| phoned-in | film & tv | 1988 |
| piffle | writing | 1890 |
| pixel peeper | visual art | 2002 |
| plot bunny | writing | 2003 |
| poetaster | writing | 1601 |
| pop art | visual art | 1956 |
| popcorn movie | film & tv | 1983 |
| potboiler | writing | 1736 |
| poverty porn | film & tv | 2000 |
| pulp fiction | writing | 1931 |
| purple prose | writing | 1901 |
| **Q** | | |
| quill-driver | writing | 1756 |
| quota quickie | film & tv | 1936 |
| **R** | | |
| rhymester | writing | 1593 |
| **S** | | |
| schlockbuster | film & tv | 1966 |
| schlock rock | music | 1968 |
| screed | writing | c. 1350 |
| scrunge | music | 1995 |
| shock art | visual art | c. 2000 |
| shoot-'em-up | film & tv | 1953 |
| slush pile | writing | 1907 |
| solecism | writing | 1577 |
| sonneteer | writing | 1667 |
| SoundCloud rap | music | 2014 |
| summer novel | writing | 1876 |
| Sunday painter | visual art | 1925 |
| **T** | | |
| tinselry | visual art | 1830 |
| tract | writing | 1806 |
| Tumblrcore | music | c. 2010 |
| twee | music | c. 1980 |
| **V** | | |
| versifier | writing | 1531 |
| **Y** | | |
| yacht rock | music | 2005 |
| yellow journalism | writing | 1897 |

*Newest term with lowest current burn.*

as a beginners' guide to an age-old craft, and reminds us that critique is very often its own form of creativity. But let it also serve as a warning—after all, there's a derisive term for seemingly every work of art. As an artist or as a consumer, you have the right to use language for the goal of making sense of a piece. Just wield it wisely and don't let it wield you.

—*Bryce Woodcock*

# SACRIFICE ZONE

## A SEMI-REGULAR GUEST COLUMN ABOUT REGULARLY IGNORED PLACES. IN THIS ISSUE: EASTWICK

*by Emma Copley Eisenberg*

*Even in the mid-twentieth century, **Eastwick** was 5,700 acres of freshwater tidal marsh in a semirural community, where vast open spaces attracted residents who wanted to live off the land, as well as weekend visitors from more densely populated parts of Philly.*

I'm standing in a patch of grass, looking across four lanes of traffic at a Kia dealership whose windows read CASH FOR CLUNKERS, and whose speakers play a voice droning "Sales line one, sales line one" loud enough for me to hear over the roar of the semitrucks and planes passing overhead. This patch of grass is in Eastwick, the southwesternmost neighborhood of Philadelphia, and the one next to mine. I'm the only person walking for a mile, so drivers turn and stare as I approach a telephone pole with prayer candles scattered around its base and a teddy bear tied to it with cord. It bears a piece of blue posterboard with the words LONG LIVE STRAWS WE LOVE YOU, GOD LOVED YOU MORE HE COULDN'T WAIT written in black Sharpie. There is an opening in the cluster of trees

Eastwick

*Photographs throughout by the author*

*I'm the only person walking for a mile, so drivers turn and stare as I approach a telephone pole with prayer candles scattered around its base and a teddy bear tied to it with cord.*

that separates where I stand from the Schuylkill River Tank Farm, where people have dumped tires, plastic bottles, and an old silver-and-black TV.

Eastwick is perhaps best known for being the Philly neighborhood that always floods (it sits between the Cobbs and Darby creeks and the Schuylkill River), and for containing part of the Philadelphia International Airport, and for this environmentally hazardous site where I now stand. The tank farm is part of the former Philadelphia Energy Solutions oil refinery, which was the biggest and oldest refinery on the East Coast and was the largest air polluter in Philadelphia until, in 2019, it exploded. Eastwick's soil and groundwater are heavily contaminated with benzene (known to cause leukemia and lymphoma, especially in children), lead, xylene, and other toxic compounds—and still contain three times the EPA's actionable level, even since the plant shut down.

Eastwick also once hosted two landfills—one of which overlooked a residential area—that also leaked industrial chemicals into the soil and groundwater, until they were closed and capped in the early 2000s.

Eastwick is Park 'N Fly asphalt lots and illegal trash dumping; it is I-95 and Cargo City, a major FedEx shipping hub; and it is George Wharton Pepper Middle School, closed in 2013 due to chronic flooding, and then abandoned. In 2018 the Philadelphia Department of Streets reportedly picked up more than twenty-six tons of garbage and five thousand used tires from the school's grounds. Eastwick, I'm seeing, is now a place where things are moved and sold, stored and forgotten. But it was not always this way.

In order for something to be sacrificed, it must first be precious. After all, in one of our most famous stories of sacrifice, it is not just anyone whom Abraham is asked to kill to prove his faith in God, but his own son. And oh, how precious Eastwick once was!

Even in the mid-twentieth century, Eastwick was 5,700 acres of freshwater tidal marsh in a semirural community, where vast open spaces attracted residents who wanted to live off the land, as well as weekend visitors from more densely populated parts of Philly. Its inhabitants included Black people, many of them descendants of formerly enslaved farmers in the South who had come north during the Great Migration; Jewish people from Eastern Europe; Italian people and Roma people. Everyone lived side by side; each family owned their own land and grew much of their own food. "A Huckleberry Finn experience," residents say, verbatim, over and over again, in a recent oral history project. "No racial strife. Pristine land. Total freedom."

They grew corn, greens, watermelons, grapes, apples, peaches, strawberries, blackberries, and medicinal herbs in Eastwick. They canned. They kept chickens; they fished. They wandered in the woods. They swam in the Delaware River.

Perhaps the city of Philadelphia did not yet know what it was sacrificing, or perhaps it did know but did not care. Unconnected to municipal infrastructure, Eastwick lacked sidewalks and sewers, and instead of looking precious to official eyes, perhaps it looked empty. In 1950, motivated by worry over suburban flight, and newly rich from postwar grant dollars, the city declared Eastwick a "blighted slum" and scheduled the neighborhood for "redevelopment." The plan

of development in Eastwick is on people's lips again, but this time residents are pushing back. No more asphalt, they say; what is needed is porous ground that can absorb water, and other long-term flooding solutions. There are multiple neighborhood advocacy associations, and meetings open to the public are often packed with residents.

From where I stand now, in 2023, on Essington Avenue, I can peer through the trees and see the squat white cylinders of the tank farm, which are connected to downtown Philadelphia by pipelines that run under the river. Eastwick is a place our city has decided is unworthy of our care, even as it has produced resources that power us all.

was to build housing complexes where the fruit trees and corn fields and woods had once been. Starting in 1957, the city used eminent domain to acquire more than two thousand homes, displacing 8,636 of the 19,300 Eastwick residents, and breaking up the shape and character of this relaxed, racially integrated community. The city literally moved earth to do this, demolishing homes and raising the elevation of low-lying Eastwick by adding eleven million cubic yards of fill dredged from the Schuylkill River.

Is anyone surprised that this plan did not create the kind of tidy, modern community the blueprints had promised? The city paved Paradise and put up poor-quality housing that, over time, became parking lots. (The fill settled strangely, causing the foundations of the new housing projects to crack and lean in and ultimately to sink; many have been left vacant, while others were purchased by the Redevelopment Authority at market value and demolished.) Or it abandoned the idea of housing altogether, turning over the land to other uses. One hundred and fifty acres of the neighborhood were allocated in 1966 to modernize the Philadelphia International Airport and to build Cargo City. Twelve hundred acres became the John Heinz National Wildlife Refuge at Tinicum.

Sewers to manage the floodwaters were never built; seven tropical storms or hurricanes between 1999 and 2021 flooded parts of Eastwick with up to five and a half feet of muddy water, a problem that is only getting worse with climate change. "Development" proceeded slowly, and eventually stalled in the 1980s due to white flight from the city, which reduced the demand for homes in the neighborhood. Eastwick is now 73 percent Black, and in 2006 it was once again declared a "blighted slum" by the Redevelopment Authority, this time while the land was still under its management. These days, the prospect

On my way home, I stop by the John Heinz National Wildlife Refuge at Tinicum, the only remaining piece of what Eastwick once looked like, and remember that I came here to see the total solar eclipse in 2017 (complete with those funny glasses). There are bald eagles and blue herons and egrets and swans living in the marshland, and here you can forget that the airport is just on the other side of a fence. Perhaps Eastwick was sacrificed because the loss was necessary for an idea, an impossible idea of our city's future that never came to pass, in which Philadelphia was magically transformed into a shiny, homogenous land of power and influence. Eastwick was, is, precious, given a different way of measuring value than the one that we have chosen—it is precious precisely because it was once wild and undeveloped, and was once a place where people lived closely together and took care of one another. But for a moment, everywhere I look, that other kind of value is visible. ★

# MONA SIMPSON

[WRITER]

"DEATH, FAILURE, DIMINISHMENT,
AND REGRET COMPEL ME NOW.
HEROISM A LITTLE LESS SO."

Some of the satisfactions of writing, according to Mona Simpson:
*Patterns that emerge on their own*
*Plot turns that come to you in dreams*
*Inevitable endings*

**B**orn in Wisconsin, Mona Simpson is descended, on her mother's side, from a Green Bay mink farmer. Her mother, Joanne Carole Schieble, was a speech pathologist who taught stroke victims to talk again, and her father was an immigrant from Syria. After her parents divorced, in 1962, Mona, then five, lost touch with her father, eventually moving to Los Angeles with her mom. She received a scholarship to the University of California at Berkeley, where she studied poetry with Leonard Michaels, Ishmael Reed, Thom Gunn, Seamus Heaney, and Josephine Miles. As Joan Didion had years earlier, Simpson won the prestigious Mademoiselle Guest Editor competition. Josephine Miles told Simpson that when Joan Didion won, she stood on top of the classroom desk, raised one arm, and said, "I'm going to New York City." Simpson would make the same move.

In her twenties, she enrolled in Columbia's MFA program and also secured a work-study position at The Paris Review, living off nine thousand dollars a year. Her

*Illustration by Kristian Hammerstad*

*teachers at Columbia included Elizabeth Hardwick, Edmund White, and* New Yorker *fiction editor Charles "Chip" McGrath. While in school, Simpson worked on her first novel,* Anywhere but Here, *and years of revision followed. It's a dexterous book about the relationship between a mother and daughter. It became a bestseller and was adapted into a film starring Natalie Portman and Susan Sarandon.*

*Since her debut, Simpson has published six more novels, including* My Hollywood *(2010) and* Casebook *(2014).* Commitment, *her newest novel, follows the lives of three children and their single mother, who struggles financially and mentally to raise them. Having steered her kids toward their dreams— ones they had, and ones she had for them—she reaches her limits, and her debilitating depression results in her being placed in an institution. The book is a portrait of a family at a pivotal moment, and an examination of the political and social constructs that can make or break an individual. Simpson is a research-driven writer, and says she will use whatever she can to make a book come alive. One feels this in* Commitment: *the characters seem to percolate on the page, their lived realities emerging in a full-bodied way.*

*Simpson and I spoke on the phone twice, corresponded by email, and grabbed dinner when she was in Manhattan. I booked a restaurant in Greenwich Village that serves family-style plates—something that ultimately proved daunting. One strives for elegance, but a slippery brussels sprout is sometimes bound to fly across the table. Plating Simpson's dish made me nervous, so I kept in mind a story from* American Hustle *and* Silver Linings Playbook *writer and director David O. Russell. He called Mona one of the most formidable minds he knew, an intense person, though in spite of her intensity, she once put on a gorilla suit for his son's birthday.*
—Yvonne Conza

### I. PECKING OUT A STORY

THE BELIEVER: What made you want to write?

MONA SIMPSON: Originally? A love of reading. Exuberance. Near poverty. Adolescent isolation. A mentally ill mom.

I started in high school, in the usual way: as a means of making something. We'd moved into an apartment with almost no furniture: only beds in the bedroom and chairs in the living room, no table. But my mother bought me a small pumpkin-colored Parsons desk and a typewriter. Late at night, I would sit at the desk and type stories. In those days, there were mandatory typing classes, but I first taught myself hunting and pecking. When I had to take the class, I was already fast. (They timed us. You had to look up while your fingers sped over the keys.)

People write for ludicrous, craven ambitions when they're sixteen. And also because it feels good to shape a tiny world out of the only tool you have at that age: your native language. And to then realize that this constructed world can feel like a refuge.

The next question may be: *What makes you want to keep writing,* as Raymond Carver once wrote, *even so?* Last year, a student asked me whether he had the talent to make it as a writer. I asked him how he defined "making it." He asked if I thought he could someday win the Nobel Prize. I told him I'd feel satisfied if, by the end of our class, he could write a great toast for his best friend's wedding.

After fifty, we write, hauling a sack of failures over our shoulder. The shine has worn off childish ambitions. But that is when the work becomes interesting.

BLVR: What does "even so" represent for you?

MS: What I mean by saying "even so" is that it's easy to write when you're so young that you're imagining your acceptance speech for the Nobel Prize. After some devastating losses of beloved people, after disappointments in yourself, that exuberance becomes tempered. Refined.

BLVR: Your mother's occupation of helping stroke victims to speak again made me think about how writing itself is learning to talk again.

MS: When I now remember my mother teaching people to talk again, it feels like a beautiful act. It was slow and laborious work, using the body (jaw, mouth, ears) and a steady infusion of hope. Stroke victims sometimes told my mother the words were inside, they just couldn't find the string to pull them out. Learning to talk again is a perfect metaphor. We're always rebuilding new lives on top of the ones we've lived. And sometimes the new life has a smaller vocabulary. But even if the size of a lexicon is diminished, its expressive power can be equal to it or stronger, with an intense effort and need.

BLVR: In many ways your oeuvre enlists a "spokes of the wheel" empathy toward the human condition: family, psychological fragmentation, money, our society's mental health crisis, the shortcomings of institutions, and more. Do you think about it in those terms?

MS: I wasn't sure what "spokes of the wheel" meant, so I googled it and found a diagram, with a hub for *empathy* in the middle and eight points outside for *intuition, focus, connect, inquisitive, solution, attention, selfless, self-aware*. I like all those qualities, though I'm still not sure exactly what you mean, but I'm certainly interested in the family, our society's mental health crisis, our lack of childcare, and the vanishing of institutions.

*My Hollywood* concerns immigrant women who take care of American children so they can send money to their own families to pay for school tuition and childcare across the ocean. It also chronicles the women who hire them, who suffer themselves in other ways, trying to make lives that matter outside their homes and young families.

My most recent book, *Commitment*, is about three children whose mother is no longer "all there." She falls into mental illness and haunts the lives of her children and her best friend, the four people who love her most. It's also about the last years of public institutions that were intended and built for the mentally ill, to provide a smaller, safer world, one in which, in the best cases, they could recover, or at least live with dignity, some happiness, and a sense of purpose and contribution.

BLVR: Was your intention to examine the national mental health crisis through this book?

MS: Yes, I think so. It was an attempt to understand, to really understand, how we treat mental illness. Mental illness has always been with us, and the long history of how we've cared for people with this infirmity is checkered and tragic. We all know about the worst extremes, when we threw people into freezing rivers or left them chained in the snow outside, but there are also some moments of idealism in the long history, records of cures, and of lives lived out with dignity and interest.

The ways we've treated mental illness have changed radically in the last fifty years. I wanted to learn whether those changes improved things for most people. But then all that makes it sound as if I've written a different kind of book. *Commitment* is a novel, which means it doesn't have an agenda. The treatment of mental illness is there, but in the background of specific lives.

I try to render the ways that a tragic fact such as a beloved mother falling ill can change the trajectory of a young man's career. How having a mother in an institution leads a young woman to feel she can't tell the truth about herself (the truth feels unexplainable) to the man she thinks she's falling in love with.

BLVR: *Commitment* has emotional impulses and thematic commonality with your other books. American characters and their yearnings for the American dream result in the examination of myths regarding the social constructs of class, families, mental illness, institutions, and more. Is it a conscious choice to have your books be in conversation with one another?

MS: I'm pleased you feel the books are in conversation with one another. I try to go deeper with each book, to risk more. Personal lives, intimate lives—influenced, if not determined, by larger political forces and social constructs—have always been the material out of which novels are made.

I've been thinking about the relative dearth of single mothers in fiction, and I'm wondering if this is because so much of what fuels plots is still the kind of romance that promises everything will be good once two people tear through the complications, confusions, and obstacles, and begin a life together. Divorce would seem to be the potion for marriage-plot poison. It is a large element of how we live, and people now live differently, when divorced, than they did in *What Maisie Knew* [the novel by Henry James]. It's up to us as storytellers to find new shapes for novels that yield pleasure, with the added depths and resonance lent by the reality of new social forms.

## II. CRAFT AND COUNSEL

BLVR: Where do you start with a story? Is there one thing that first captivates your attention?

MS: Usually it's something nerdy and verbal. A vernacular phrase. A bit of slang. A voice can make a character

# DIASPORIC

*by Michael Prior*

Like Boccaccio's idle rich, we tell ourselves stories
to avoid admitting we can't
go back. The islands in my mind,
vaster than this island on a map.
Here, rain's meticulous patina. Here,
the walled garden's scattered windfall,
a copper stag greening on a hill,
the colorful names for local waterfowl:
shags, eiders, divers, moorhens
skirting the skeins of the River Esk.
None of this is mine, only borrowed,
like the book I've brought
in which radiant Genji—allusive, elusive—
tosses off verse after verse
about a dying season, while failing to imagine
pain beyond his own.
Where I grew up, or failed to, hawkweed burned
along the Fraser, the Strait's

capricious hues. There, I overheard a language
I never learned, countless stories
of a camp, a war, a seiner, a delta wracked by loss
written into law. Which of them
remain true? When the night sky churns itself
clear and starry after a deluge.
When a wasp polishes its own striped coffin
and, exhausted, turns circles
on the sill—*Then, is there a way forward if not back?*
asked a friend. Another, wondered
why I didn't write haiku. To say Genji,
barring time and temerity, was cruel,
say, *I'm too far removed*, or *It's raining now*.
Say that the lessons I took but couldn't finish
began with questions: *Nani? Itsu?*
*Dare? Doko?* Say that inside return's false dream
each glittering memory, each scrap
of voice, unfurls itself a hole.

---

for me. Later on, I have to remember to consider what they look like.

BLVR: Was your poetry background influential with respect to your voice and confidence as a writer?

MS: I don't know. One can be an insecure poet just as easily as one can be an insecure novelist. But I think poetry did give me a sense of how to enter a story. From poetry, I know how to look for the sentence that can be a door. In poetry, the line is an essential unit; that compression teaches you to recognize sentences with a hook in them.

BLVR: When you first started publishing, did you have a submission strategy?

MS: My first published story was in *The Iowa Review*. My friend Rob [Robert Cohen] had had a story accepted by them. So within a few days, the rest of Rob's friends and I (we were all in Columbia's MFA program) submitted stories to that same editor. It feels generous to call this a "strategy." Perhaps "pack mentality" fits better. Or "frantic opportunism."

BLVR: How key is top-tier placement of stories to a writer's career? Any smaller publications you'd recommend?

MS: There are so many good magazines when it comes to stories: *n+1*, *The Yale Review*, *Granta*, *Joyland*, and *Harper's Magazine*, to name just a few. What George Plimpton used to say when I worked at *The Paris Review* was that we had only eight thousand subscriptions but they were the right eight thousand. What he meant was that editors, agents, and writers all read the periodical.

BLVR: The copyright page of *Anywhere but Here* mentions that some stories in the book were originally published in different publications. Were those individual stories—"Approximations," "What My Mother Knew," and "Lonnie Tishman"—always linked to writing *Anywhere but Here*?

MS: I wrote "Approximations" as a short story. I can tell, all these years later, because it's structured as a child's struggle to hold on to her father and resist the new stepfather. The story ends with some hope for her connection with the stepfather, whom the reader recognizes as the man who's there. "What My Mother Knew" and "Lonnie Tishman" came later, excerpts drawn from the novel. "Coins" started as a stand-alone story, too, which grew into *My Hollywood*.

BLVR: What continues to draw you back to short stories?

MS: I love the myth of the short story: that everything can change forever in one charged moment. That an insight can alter the whole subsequent course of a life.

As a reader, I regularly return to I. B. Singer, Alice Munro, Grace Paley, and Chekhov for the satisfactions of an elegant shape and a thrilling ending.

BLVR: There's something you stated earlier that I'd like to better understand. "*Commitment* is a novel, which means it doesn't have an agenda." What does that mean?

MS: It means that whatever I say a novel is "about" feels somehow a little false to my own ear, as if I'm responding to a question on the radio, because novels don't work on the engine of arguments and examples. They're always insufficient in description.

BLVR: One of your early roles at *The Paris Review* was writing rejection letters. What went into the crafting of them?

MS: We had two different "form" rejection slips we used for work that didn't excite us; I wrote only to the subset of writers whose work felt promising. I owed these writers a thoughtful and honest response. I found it to be a perfect job. For long afternoons, I sat in an old chair by the office's one window and read, as snow fell outside or blossoms blew to the pavement. Years later, I met some of the writers with whom I'd corresponded, and these were always poignant meetings, because we'd shared an intimacy without really knowing each other at all.

BLVR: What advice do you have for a writer when a book review gets it wrong?

MS: Writers have very little recourse to misunderstanding. A prizewinning writer wrote about reading a crushing review from someone he very much admired, someone he'd hoped would like his book. There's something that feels so personal about all this. And it doesn't just feel personal; it is personal. Reading a book involves collaboration, deep involvement. There are critics I admire who have never written about my work. It's like hoping to be asked to dance. It feels sad—one believes one could learn from a critic one takes seriously—and yet I'm glad George Eliot didn't "learn from" what Henry James wrote about *Middlemarch*.

I just came from the *Manet/Degas* show [at the Metropolitan Museum of Art], which has taken New York by storm, and I'm sure that's because of the brilliant curation, which reveals the personal narratives of the two artists. Though they were only two years apart in age, Degas clearly looked up to Manet. He drew and painted the more famous artist's portrait many times (and also Mrs. Manet's); he mentioned Manet in his letters to other people and through his life; he collected and restored Manet's paintings. Manet never once drew or painted Degas. One night, after Degas had dinner with the Manets, he went home and painted a scene of them in their home: Manet in repose; Manet's wife, Suzanne, at the piano. He offered them the painting as a gift, and Manet violently slashed the canvas with a knife, cutting off Mrs. Manet's face.

We don't know more about what transpired, but Degas kept this damaged portrait he'd made of his friend, painting over the gash with a neutral monochrome panel. It's interesting that he didn't try to remake the incomplete portrait over the damage. Like any inequality of affection, it's painful.

The curator of the exhibition told me that in France, because the exhibit was presented as a pairing, the French press immediately considered it a competition. In their assessment, Manet won. In my assessment, Degas wins.

BLVR: Are established writers getting a fair shake in today's marketplace?

MS: If established writers aren't getting a fair shake, then who is? Do you mean that we have an appetite for the new? I once gave a beloved niece (who is also an intelligent reader) a volume by Alice Munro, which she loved. A few years later, she was asking me what books she should take along on a trip. I gave her a list and also mentioned that Munro had a new book out. She said she'd already read her.

Personally, I'm satisfied with subtler gradations of novelty. I was thrilled when one could open a magazine and find a new Munro or a new Trevor or a new Carver or Wolff.

I still feel that way when I find a new Deborah Eisenberg. A new Bryan Washington. A new Yiyun Li.

BLVR: Where should writers turn their attention while building their careers?

MS: Maybe the most important corners for literary writers in today's marketplace are the independent bookstores. Independent bookstores serve a central role in the development of serious readers that is not addressed by Amazon or any other online purveyor. Readers can go into an independent bookstore and have a real conversation about a book with a bookseller who is well read enough to lead them to unfamiliar work that holds some of the pleasures they've enjoyed, while also, sometimes, setting a greater challenge.

So many people learn to read for pleasure in college. In literature classes, you have the excitement of discussing a book slowly, hearing other people's ideas about it, and learning about the context in which it was written, how it came about, what strains of society are reflected in its background. Once you leave campus and go out into the world, many ex-English majors miss this kind of conversation. I've thought of starting a Substack reading group called "I was an English major" for people to congregate and read with care. George Saunders is doing that, in his Story Club. But novels and poems could also benefit from this kind of intricate conversation.

BLVR: What's your biggest takeaway from an editor?

MS: Ann Close, my editor for most of my career, influenced me enormously. Sadly, Ann decided to retire this year; we celebrated her in mid-December, after her last day of work at Alfred A. Knopf. She would go down to the floor where the production editors collated the writers' marks on the copyedited manuscript. She'd call and say, "You're taking the life out of this book." Or: "You cut this line from the third draft. I liked that line." Another time, when I was struggling with the demotic of Lola's voice in *My Hollywood*, she said, "Well, she wouldn't think in English." Of course, that was right. We all think in our first language. So I used her musical, half-made-up English in her dialogue, but let her thoughts unspool fluently.

### III. "CHARACTERS LIVE IN SPECIFIC ROOMS"

BLVR: In the escalating climate of censorship, cancel culture, and book banning, would today's trigger warnings regarding incest have diluted the powerful tensions in *Lawns*, published in 1984?

MS: Is there such a thing as a spoiler-sensitive trigger warning? In general, I wonder if fragility is best protected or challenged, but that's probably for every reader to decide for herself. When I find myself feeling acutely sensitive, it's sometimes more useful to push myself into uncomfortable situations, because otherwise it can feel like I'm living in a smaller and smaller world.

BLVR: *Lawns'* origins link to your freelance journalist days. You interviewed circus performers, Buddhist bakers, a dim sum chef, performance artists, a woman leading an incest victims' group.

MS: For the incest piece, I interviewed doctors, perpetrators, victims, siblings of victims, mothers of victims, people who

were victims years ago, and more. The story on incest treatment was printed in the *San Francisco Chronicle*'s Sunday magazine, and I think it even won a prize. My longtime editor there, Jane Ciabattari, a writer herself, later went to *Redbook* and bought the story "Lawns." In the end, *Redbook* wanted me to make the mother's character more heroic, and that didn't feel quite right, so then I sent it to *The Iowa Review*.

BLVR: What was important to you in telling that story?

MS: I think what mattered to me most was telling a story of the young woman's struggle and resilience and her eventual integration of a tragic past into a promising life.

BLVR: Were you concerned that it would be eroticized? That readers would be upset? Though, shouldn't they be? Isn't discomfort an element of fiction?

MS: I didn't really think this story would be eroticized, or that it would give cheap erotic pleasure—if that's what you mean. Because the young woman, a college student, has, for the first time, a sweet, fragile romance that I, and I hoped the reader, would root for.

BLVR: Does the cancel culture and censorship tinderbox, with potential blowback, affect what you write?

MS: No one wants to be canceled. But we don't want to be tepid either.

BLVR: For writers who, like me, are grappling with subjects of incest, suicide, and other gray-zone topics, in what ways can we retain our vision without having our creative choices constrained or censored?

MS: Frightening material in fiction can help us make sense of our lives. I'm working on a piece that includes suicide. If someone chooses not to read it, that's all right. But I'm going to write it.

BLVR: In November 2018, your short story "Wrong Object," published by *Harper's Magazine*, was included in *The Best American Short Stories 2019*, edited by Anthony Doerr. He remarked that it "pushes the reader to a different frontier of empathy—pedophilia—but by the end of [the] story, you might be surprised to find yourself asking: Who among us can't relate to trying to repel our own unbidden desires?" Did you receive any pushback from editors on the story?

MS: No. The editor at *Harper's Magazine* was very thoughtful.

BLVR: Do you think it's important for writers to be able to approach topical social issues?

MS: I don't usually think of stories as pieces on topical social issues. I wonder if social issues don't sometimes coalesce and become clear to us after they've been written about in fiction. In other words, maybe social issues as we know them and name them follow literature, rather than the other way around. I think fiction writers tend to write from inside a character's consciousness. And of course, characters live in specific rooms, in specific times and places, so whatever injustices and miseries exist in their culture touch them or don't, depending on where they're situated in their society. I'm thinking of *Sentimental Education*, of Becky Sharp from *Vanity Fair: A Novel Without a Hero*, even of *Middlemarch*. Complicated characters are really the only ones that interest us.

### IV. THE PRIVILEGE OF INTIMACY

BLVR: Your next book, *Help and Its Sequel*, is based on your early years in New York and will explore the challenges of helping people. Why is the timing right to publish this material right now?

MS: I'm writing this book, as I've written all my previous books, before selling it. Which is another way of saying that I have no idea if the "timing is right" for this material. But the timing feels right for me to be writing this story. I've thought about much of the material for a long time, and I'm only now beginning to understand it, to begin to see the scenes as rooms in a house.

BLVR: Has your definition of success changed from book to book, over your lifetime?

MS: I try not to think in terms of success or failure. Those words are too broad, like off and on switches or blunt hammers on aspirations as fine as thread. We have so few real metrics with which to judge fiction, and none of them really work. There are sales figures and bestseller lists. There are prizes. None of them prove to be accurate predictors of what lasts. (If you have any doubt, google who won the Nobel Prize in Literature in 1919, when Proust was eligible and did not receive it. Or in 1928, after *To the Lighthouse* was published.) For almost any major prize, the list of writers who were eligible but didn't receive it is more impressive than the list of winners.

The longer you write, too, you learn to find many satisfactions within the work itself. Patterns emerge on their own. Plot turns come to you in dreams. Endings feel inevitable by the time you come to them. The work begins to give back to you.

I try to do what I can—those famous late words of Henry James, "We work in the dark—we do what we can—we give what we have. Our doubt is our passion and our passion is our task. The rest is the madness of art."

BLVR: Factual details from your own life can be found throughout your work. In *Commitment*, Lina, like you, had a fondness for wearing overalls, throwing clay pottery, and working in an ice cream shop. How do you think about the autobiographical entering your fiction?

MS: How did you know I was once a potter, Yvonne? I was raised to be an artistic prodigy, and so I came to failure early. My mother hoped to raise a musician. She sent me to

---

## MALE AUTHORS ACCUSED OF STEALING WORK FROM THEIR WIVES

* F. Scott Fitzgerald, from Zelda Fitzgerald
* Ted Hughes, from Carol Orchard
* Ted Hughes, from Sylvia Plath
* Robert Browning, from Elizabeth Barrett Browning
* Percy Bysshe Shelley, from Mary Shelley
* Henry Gauthier-Villars, from Colette
* William Wordsworth, from Mary Hutchinson
* T. S. Eliot, from Vivienne Haigh-Wood Eliot

*—list compiled by Claire Fairtlough*

Interlochen, the Michigan music camp, when I was seven years old. My grandmother kept the letters I sent home: "Please come and get me." I took a class called Musical Talent Exploration, in which children rotated between every instrument in the orchestra, while supervising adults, presumably, watched, alert for signs of giftedness. I don't think many were detected in me. I wanted to play the string bass, but I was a small child so they gave me a viola, which I played—not prodigiously—for the next decade.

In terms of my life coming into fiction, those misadventures can be useful. I like the details: the smell of rosin, the technicalities of scooping a three-ounce ball of ice cream. Of course, when one hasn't had an experience oneself, one can always research. For two years after college, I worked writing press releases at an arts organization by day, but I spent my free time and all my energy freelancing as a journalist. I loved driving around California and interviewing people. I did a two-part piece on the emergency room of the hospital where San Francisco's indigent population was treated; I did a feature on happy housewives (despite second-wave feminism), and as you know, another long piece on incest treatment. I found I loved the interviews and the research more than the endpieces, because often, what interested me most ended up on the cutting-room floor.

Doing research for fiction allows you to keep exactly those bits you love. I did a lot of research for *Commitment* at Metropolitan State Hospital in Norwalk, California, the closest mental health hospital still open near where I live, and I learned a great deal from three retired nurses who worked there for most of their professional lives and who still volunteer, putting the hospital archives in order. The land itself is suggestive with its vast variety of old trees that look in need of tending.

BLVR: Have you retained the "exactly three ounces" scoop skill?

MS: No, but I still have strange cravings involving ice cream. Last summer we sliced stone fruit, baked the slices, and served them with coconut ice cream.

BLVR: In getting to know you, I'm struck by your resilience. Where does it come from?

MS: Scientists believe that resilience issues from alleles in our DNA sequences. If so, I've been lucky. People who live through frightening childhoods can find the adult world more comprehensible, and kinder, than the dangers they once believed were real. I still feel the relief and happiness I first discovered in having an apartment of my own, or later in being able to make a middle-class living. I learned to cook and found real pleasure in having friends, staying up late even when we were all tired, because our conversation, with laughter and middle-of-the-night revelations, was too irresistible to stop.

BLVR: At this stage in your life, what about your work has become most interesting to you?

MS: For years, I worked late at night, early in the morning, while everyone in the house was sleeping. My children are young adults now, and I teach lightly, so I have the luxury of letting a book swallow a whole day. I've been able to loosen myself, and my interests in the world have exploded. A lot of young work is about finding a way to live.

By middle age, one has experienced death, up close and personally. I've lost people I believed I couldn't live without, and yet here I am. With the vantage of age, the shapes of lives become visible, beautiful, and poignant. Death, failure, diminishment, and regret compel me now. Heroism a little less so. Age makes everyone a Buddhist.

BLVR: I'm feeling very Buddhist with my sixtieth birthday coming up. It's an age that pinches a nerve about where I am in my career. What nurtures and sustains your creative talents?

MS: I promise turning sixty is OK, especially when you look the way you do.

Reading. Friends. My dog. Walks. Birds. Kindness. A garden. I have two children, who are joys and redemptions. I've fallen in love in what used to be thought of as old age. I feel grateful to share work with friends whose work I admire, to teach books I love to students, from whom I learn about being young in the twenty-first century.

BLVR: Aside from working with those

students, and learning from them, what do you hope to accomplish that's unrelated to your own writing?

MS: I want to garden more. I'd like to become closer to the people I work with. I hope to sustain a good marriage. I wish my community were more diverse in terms of age and experience. I've always been a bit of an ageist, preferring people my own age. That won't work so well, going forward.

BLVR: Is there a highlight of your literary career that stands out?

MS: People in an independent bookstore baked a cake with a perfect replica of my book cover on it. Once, another bookstore made a float for me to ride in. Who says this work isn't glamorous? But of course, the measurement of one's "career" and "highlights" is subjective. I write books. I have a good day when a few pages come out well. Recently, a friend described his experience of reading *Commitment*, and listening to him made me so happy. He'd experienced what I'd hoped the book could do, in a way that would be hard for me to articulate. Readers are sometimes the best interpreters of our work. After talks, people have come to ask me about something very specific in a book that connected to their lives. That kind of intimacy feels like a privilege and a reward.

BLVR: Along the lines of a final intimacy: Can you tell us something about your writing life that has surprised you?

MS: Once, when my son was in third or fourth grade, I overheard one boy say to another about [that kid's] dad's book: "I hear his book sucks." After that, I started dreading publication. My kids had watched me work days and years; they'd both given up things for Mom's work. I thought it would embarrass them to hear that their mom's book sucked. It could make them feel foolish for having believed in my dream, for having sacrificed to support it. But it turned out not to be that way at all. My grown children drag their friends to readings. That relief is just one of the many various deep pleasures of having adult children. ★

# THE WAY BACK

### A NEW ROTATING GUEST COLUMN OF WRITERLY REMEMBRANCES
### IN THIS ISSUE: SUTTON PLACE, 1970

*by Daniel Halpern*

In August 1970, I arrived in New York City with five dollars, a broken hand in an Italian cast, and a phone number, given to me by a friend in Tangier, of a woman who loved to cook Moroccan food. I called the number, and Paula Wolfert, who would become one of the most beloved cookbook writers in America, answered. I told her I'd just come from Tangier, where I'd been living and working on *Antaeus*, a new literary magazine, with Paul Bowles. She said to come meet her and maybe she could help me. She lived in a nice building on East Seventy-Second Street.

We talked about Tangerine friends and, of course, the local food there. She was working on her iconic Moroccan cookbook *Couscous and Other Good Food from Morocco*. She said I was welcome to stay in her apartment for the next month, as she would be vacationing out of town. I'm not sure what I would have done at that point, being penniless and knowing no one in the city.

When Paula returned in September, she introduced me to her friend Loretta Foye, a tough Irish computer expert, brought up in Red Hook, who had a huge heart and a large apartment in Chelsea with an extra bedroom. Her friends were bartenders, taxi drivers, cops, and chefs. She agreed to let me stay there rent-free if I cleaned the apartment once a week, fed her five cats (I wasn't allergic yet), and shared a room with her pet green snake, which lived in a modest terrarium that seemed secure. I hate snakes, green or otherwise. I think it ate lettuce and insects, but I'm not sure. I was tempted to let it play with the cats. Anyway, it was a silent roommate.

Loretta had a boyfriend, a large Italian chef who worked at a decent restaurant on Lexington. She and I never had any kind of romantic relationship, but she was incredibly kind to me. She volunteered to have dinners for my new friends to help me get established in New York City. She fought against my natural reticence, and told me that if I was going to remain in New York and be any kind of success, I needed to find a way to be a little more demonstrative, by which she meant that my level of ambition was below her expectations. Actually, I had plenty of ambition; it just remained slightly indirect. Loretta was sweetly sentimental. Some nights I'd come home and she'd be sitting in her living room with a glass of Irish whiskey, neat, listening to Frank Sinatra and weeping gently. My Black Irish landlord.

Every Friday, Loretta held forth at a dinner at a bar-restaurant on Third Avenue called Caliban. Always a varied group. My favorite guest from Loretta's weekly table was a woman named Gretchen, a professional contortionist. I'm not sure how the professional part worked; there might have been a circus involved in her past. We hung out for a few months.

Years later I tracked down Loretta, who was living in Brooklyn. This is where writing about the past gets interesting—what you remember, what another remembers, and what really happened, which doesn't matter. I had in mind to ask her if I'd made up the green snake. It seemed so odd that she'd have had one, but as odd that I'd have made it up. I got my answer, and instead of revising and correcting what I wrote earlier, I'm leaving it in, in the spirit of Rashomon. And adding in Loretta's memory, for two reasons. It's definitely more accurate, and also it's a better story.

Loretta said, "I never had a green snake! With five cats? And who would want to live with a snake? But there was a green snake who stayed with us for a while. It belonged to a woman you met at one of my dinners. She was a contortionist and you liked her. She was pretty and clearly agile. For some reason, I remember your conversation. You asked her what she did and she told you she was a contortionist. You asked—rudely, I thought—if she worked in a circus.

*Illustration by Rich Tommaso*

'No,' she said. And so you, again rudely, asked, 'What does a contortionist do, then?' She said, 'Do you want to find out?' And I remember exactly how you responded: 'Yes, I do.' But to answer your question about the green snake, it was the contortionist's snake, and she took it everywhere with her, in some sort of reptile carrier." A better story.

My goal was to continue *Antaeus*, and I needed to find funding. Every morning I walked from the apartment on Twenty-Second Street to my box at the General Post Office, across from Penn Station, stopping at a Puerto Rican bodega to get a twenty-five-cent cone of fried chicken gizzards with plenty of salt, for the walk. Getting mail was the most exciting part of the day. In fact, I might have started the magazine in order to get mail. I felt true excitement going through the letters—submissions to a magazine that had no funding for its second issue, which would include W. S. Merwin, Anne Sexton, John Berryman, Lawrence Durrell, William S. Burroughs, Muriel Rukeyser, Joyce Carol Oates, Tennessee Williams, all of whom I wrote to for material, using Bowles's name. And always there was the growing volume of unsolicited manuscripts. The first issue had arrived in New York, if not exactly "hitting the stands."

One day as I fanned the mail, a letter appeared with a green pickle in the top left corner. I did recognize the H. J. Heinz logo and immediately read the brief note. Drue Heinz wanted to subscribe to the magazine and enclosed an eight-dollar check, made out to *Antaeus*. I took the check, and a few others that had floated in, to a local Chemical Bank, and spoke with one of the younger officers. He explained that I needed to open an account to cash the check, but whatever was required, I didn't have. Mr. Brady was a kind banker, but was unable to help me without some financial history, of which I had none. I didn't even have a driver's license, and realized that if I was found dead in the street, I would end up in a place I didn't know about then, New York City's potter's field. Unidentified and unclaimed.

More checks started coming in, even though the magazine was being sold in only one bookstore, Andreas Brown's Gotham Book Mart. He had agreed to store the nine-hundred-copy first edition, as a friend of Paul's. I was able to get a handful of copies from time to time, but he would never give me a tally of the sales. Eventually it worked out. I opened up an account at the store and charged books

several times a week that I never paid for. I believe I got the better end of the deal. I spent hours in that store, in the heart of the Diamond District, talking with the elegant and mysterious Miss Steloff, the original owner, who stayed mostly in the occult books section. She was the archetypal independent bookseller, who fought to stock the controversial books of James Joyce, D. H. Lawrence, and Henry Miller.

I returned to Mr. Brady at Chemical Bank with a handful of eight-dollar subscription checks. "Look, Dan, you need some kind of financial paperwork—don't you even have a savings account?" I did not. Mr. Brady seemed sad, but said there was nothing he could do. There were rules, even then.

More checks arrived, although I knew I was taking a chance if I cashed them when there was no guarantee of *Antaeus* 2, let alone *Antaeus* 3 or 4. But for some reason, I always had a powerful, if unfounded, belief that things would be OK.

I wrote to Mr. Heinz, before I learned the writer was Mrs. Heinz, and thanked her for the subscription but said I was not sure there would be another issue, since Paul Bowles had subsidized only the first issue. She wrote back, "Let's meet and discuss. I've been looking for a literary magazine to back, and my friends have mentioned *Antaeus*, and that Paul Bowles is involved. The first issue is very good. I'm having a few people over on Saturday. Why don't you come and we can discuss this further. 8 p.m., 452 East 52nd St."

So I arrived in my Tangier uniform, jeans and a dark blue T-shirt. It was a formal type of building with various doormen, who looked askance at my outfit when I mentioned I was there for Mrs. Heinz's party. They directed me to an attended elevator, where there was another man in uniform. Before we could start up, an elderly woman rushed into the elevator. Maybe she didn't rush. She got off at her floor and we continued up. The elevator man gave me a questioning look. "What?" I asked him. He had a kindly face. "Do you know who that was?" No. I imagined he was checking out my jeans. "That was Greta Garbo." I thought, I need to remember that.

I walked out of the elevator and a woman, again in uniform, looked at my uniform and asked if I was there for the party. I was. She said it was up the staircase and pointed, although there was only one staircase. I started up and immediately saw at the top Nelson Rockefeller talking with then mayor John Lindsay. In black tie. Clearly I was in the wrong place, and I turned to retreat, but a server was coming up behind me with a salver of drinks and I had no choice but to top the stairs. I slipped past the mayor and soon-to-be vice president into a very large, elaborately decorated loft-like room. It was a formal party, and given my state of dress, I felt like I was in one of those dreams where you find yourself onstage without clothes or notes.

As luck would have it, I ran into one person I knew, Renata Adler, with whom I'd had dinner a few times when I first arrived in the city. She was wearing black hot pants and had Warren Beatty in tow—she was dating him. We three penetrated the room. On a couch was Truman Capote, asleep on Lillian Hellman's breast. Keith Richards was in a corner talking with someone who looked like Norman Mailer. Warren brought us over to see Dudley Moore, who was seeing, maybe secretly, Tuesday Weld, who had arrived and sent up word to Dudley that she was downstairs in a cab and needed him to come down and pay for it.

All in all, a breathtaking evening, an evening that might have been merely imagined. And, true to my dilemma with closure, I never did meet Drue Heinz that night.

She called me in the morning and asked if I'd been at the party. She must have seen me, but probably thought I was someone else. She asked me the status of *Antaeus 2*. It was at the printer, waiting for payment before going to press. Three thousand dollars. "My driver will bring over a check to cover the cost. Then you and I must have lunch tomorrow to sort out the details of my involvement. Let's meet at the Isle of Capri on Third Avenue, 1 p.m."

I brought the three-thousand-dollar check, along with the collection of eight-dollar subscription checks, back to Mr. Brady. He looked at me hard, clearly befuddled and suspicious. "Just a minute, Dan." And he disappeared into one of the back offices. He returned with some papers. "I vouched for you. Don't do anything strange." And I had my first checking account, age twenty-five. And that was the end of the beginning. ✶

---

## A COMPILATION OF LAST WORDS FROM HOLLYWOOD'S MOST KILLED-OFF ACTOR, SEAN BEAN

✶ *Caravaggio* (1986): "For you… For *us*."

✶ *Lorna Doone* (1990): "Ensie!"

✶ *The Field* (1990): "Stop, Da! Nobody betrayed you!"

✶ *Clarissa* (1991): "Clarissa, let this redeem my sins."

✶ *Patriot Games* (1992): "That's not my mission!"

✶ *Scarlett* (1994): "Fancy the consequences of that for you, madame."

✶ *GoldenEye* (1995): "For England, James?"

✶ *Airborne* (1998): "It's all done with, Bill. Mr. Melo is—"

✶ *Essex Boys* (2000): "I thought we were mates. I looked after you in prison."

✶ *Don't Say a Word* (2001): "Absolutely. It's mine."

✶ *The Lord of the Rings: The Fellowship of the Ring* (2001): "I would have followed you, my brother. My captain. My king."

✶ *Equilibrium* (2002): "A heavy cost. I pay it gladly."

✶ *Henry VIII* (2003): "God bless the one Catholic Church of England."

✶ *The Island* (2005): "I brought you into this world… and I can take you out of it."

✶ *Far North* (2007): "Oh, God. God, no! No! No! No! No! No! No! No! No!"

✶ *Outlaw* (2007): "'Rubbish,' he says. Eh? Rubbish! You know, Monroe? You know something? I've never heard you swear. Takes a lot of doing for a man in your shoes."

✶ *The Hitcher* (2007): "Feels good, doesn't it?"

✶ *Red Riding: The Year of Our Lord 1974* (2009): "Fuckin' hell, I'm no angel."

✶ *Black Death* (2010): "God is restored."

✶ *Death Race 2* (2010): "Good for you, Luke."

✶ *Ca$h* (2010): "I'll fucking kill you both!"

✶ *Game of Thrones* (2011): "Joffrey Baratheon is the one true heir to the Iron Throne, by the grace of all the gods, lord of the Seven Kingdoms, and protector of the realm."

✶ *Age of Heroes* (2011): "You go, I'll cover you!"

*—list compiled by Bryce Woodcock*

# CRAZY LIKE A FOX AND CLOUDLAND REVISITED

## BY S. J. PERELMAN

I could have sworn that the humorist S. J. Perelman was one of those Saul Bellow protagonists who came from Russia or Poland on a boat and took New York City by storm using the strength of his wit alone. But as it turns out, Sidney Joseph—not Seymour Joshua, as I had imagined—Perelman was born in 1904, in Brooklyn, New York, and made it big on both coasts by never saying "New York City" when "the Big Apple" was up for grabs. He was the kind of writer who thought nothing of setting a bit in an immigrant butcher shop where what's butchered (get it?) is the English language, or titling a story "Psst, Partner, Your Peristalsis Is Showing."

Two new Library of America editions of Perelmania, *Crazy Like a Fox* and *Cloudland Revisited*, aim to introduce the humorist and his zany shtick to a new generation of readers. Though he pokes fun at publications, especially the obscure and overspecialized ones, many of the pieces collected here were originally published in magazines only slightly less parochial in their tastes than *Oral Hygiene*.

Here's a not-atypical example, from "Beauty and the Bee": "Both the *Corset and Underwear Review* and the *American Bee Journal* are concerned with honeys; although I am beast enough to prefer a photograph of a succulent nymph in satin Lastex Girdleiere with Thrill Plus Bra to the most dramatic snapshot of an apiary, each has its place in my scheme."

If this frenetic Yankee style was promoted to demonstrate that Americans were, unlike their godless Soviet counterparts, true individuals—a special "overseas" edition of *Crazy Like a Fox* was published for American soldiers in 1944—it likewise demonstrated precisely the opposite, laying bare the air-conditioned nightmare of a consumer society where Lastex Girdleieres and Thrill Plus Bras seemed to enjoy a more real existence than the average Perelman.

I confess that I've always been brand-shy and am loath to drop trademarks; even writing the words "He entered a

> **Publisher:** *Library of America* **Page count:** *312* (Crazy Like a Fox*); 250* (Cloudland Revisited*)* **Price:** *$15.95* **Key quote:** *"You may be a bore to your own family, but you're worth your weight in piastres to the picture business."* **Shelve next to:** *Groucho Marx, Jean Shepherd, Mickey Spillane* **Unscientifically calculated reading time:** *Two crowns, three cavities, or one very long root canal*

Chick-fil-A" at one time required me to gird my loins. But Mr. Perelman never seems to experience any qualms on this front, and he embraces the commercial swarm rather unsqueamishly. Though you'll come across terms like *beldam*, *cacoëthes*, *objurgation*, and *coryphée* in these pages, Perelman was equally fluent in the stilted argot of comic books and hardboiled gumshoe-ese, embracing the full spectrum of what Adam Gopnik labels "American vulgarity." Words beget words, syllepsis begets syllepsis: the Julian calendar turns into an old acquaintance named Julian Callender, the evening's violet hush turns into a seductive companion named (what else?) Violet Hush, and walking past rows of female film extras turns into a stroll down Mammary Lane.

The other register on display here can be summarized only as erudite kvetching—a dry, collegiate sense of humor, perpetually put-upon, that reminded me of the kinds of conversations no doubt occurring around this time in the more polite parts of suburban St. Louis. It's a less hip forerunner of the improbable style Woody Allen came up with in *New Yorker* pieces like "The Whore of Mensa." Recalling his youthful adventures in pulp fiction—from tales like *The Mystery of Dr. Fu-Manchu* to silent films like the Lillian Gish picture *Way Down East*—Perelman manages, in his *Cloudland* columns, to evoke the heady formative years of an artist's life, with all its strange joys and intimacies intact.

To re-read Perelman is to return emphatically to another time: a time when magazines had money to spend on writers, when readers were well read, or at least read widely, and humor writing was an occupation that could support a family of four.

The jokes may be cheap, but at least the humorist usually gets the last laugh. "There is practically no problem so simple," Perelman writes, "that it cannot confuse a dentist."

—*Daniel Elkind*

*Illustration by Pete Gamlen*

A REVIEW OF

# PAGES OF MOURNING

## BY DIEGO GERARD MORRISON

Diego Gerard Morrison's winding, meta-fictional *Pages of Mourning* is both haunted and haunting. Some of the novel's ghosts are Mexico's disappeared—people who may or may not be dead, who may or may not return. The novel opens in Mexico City in 2017, just before the third anniversary of the mass kidnapping of forty-three students from Ayotzinapa Rural Teachers' College, a real case that remains unsolved. Resounding across *Pages of Mourning* is the protest cry "Vivos se los llevaron, vivos los queremos": "Alive they were taken, alive we want them back." The protagonist, Aureliano Más the Second, can relate to this sentiment. His mother vanished without explanation more than thirty years earlier, when he was an infant; he grapples with the possibility that she might in fact be long dead.

Other ghosts are literary: Aureliano hails from Comala, the literal ghost town in Juan Rulfo's novel *Pedro Páramo*, and shares a first name with nineteen characters in *One Hundred Years of Solitude*, the most famous work of magical realism. His surname, meanwhile, is a nod to his American expat mother's overidentification with Oedipa Maas of *The Crying of Lot 49*. She chose the alias Édipa Más shortly after arriving in Comala.

Despite the book's abundant references to magical realism, Aureliano, who is attempting to write a novel about his mother's disappearance, is critical of the genre. He sees it as pure fantasy, and questions its purpose in a country riven by unending cycles of cartel violence and forced disappearances, a country that chooses not to confront the likely deaths of the tens of thousands of people who have gone missing.

In pairing these literary specters with the ghosts of Mexico's drug wars, Gerard Morrison explores the stories this superstitious country tells itself about death and loss. Through this reckoning with the tendency to "put a scrim of language between [one]self and the brute reality of what's occurring," *Pages of Mourning* takes us on a formally inventive tour through Mexico's nightmares that looks straight into the face of death.

The novel begins with Aureliano's stalled attempt to use fiction to "unearth those that might already be dead." Beyond the thick cloud of allusions and questions that overshadows his life, Aureliano is stymied by his alcoholism and a related tendency to see ghosts. At his desk in a Mexico City studio, provided to him by his writing fellowship, Aureliano finds himself in an endless editing session with his dead friend Chris. He used to spend whole afternoons drinking rye-spiked espresso at a café with Chris, who painted his manuscript with red ink. "Sorry to break it to you, writer, but there don't seem to be many narrative possibilities in this literary cul-de-sac you've gotten yourself into," ghost Chris says.

Aureliano might be stuck, but Gerard Morrison has no trouble exploding narrative possibilities. Soon enough, Aureliano's aunt Rose—his mother's stepsister and an accomplished novelist—hands him her own attempt at explaining Édipa's disappearance. It's a tale that transports us back to the 1980s, when Édipa was a young runaway fleeing the California desert. She finds herself joining Rose and Aureliano's father at the top of a drug scheme peddling exclusive strains of pot to exclusive customers. This work is bound to attract cartel attention, giving rise to the paranoia that defines both Édipa and her namesake, while providing clues as to why she might have left. But though grounded in fact, Rose's story is just that—a story. Later we hear Aureliano's father's version, which is similarly unreliable. Yet these stories are the only resources Aureliano has to help him understand his mother and her choice.

This book of books has an empty center, standing in for all "those that are nowhere to be found." Ultimately, *Pages of Mourning* reckons with how to make meaning out of life when resolution remains forever out of reach, and with how to mourn—how to move forward in time—when there is no body to bury.

—*Kristen Martin*

**Publisher:** *Two Dollar Radio* **Page count:** *320* **Price:** $19.95 **Key quote:** "*In Mexico, nobody ever dies, right? We never let the dead die.*" **Shelve next to:** *Juan Rulfo, Roberto Bolaño, Thomas Pynchon, Fernanda Melchor* **Unscientifically calculated reading time:** *A whole afternoon spent pounding back double espresso shots spiked with rye whiskey*

*Illustration by Pete Gamlen*

A REVIEW OF

# ANTIQUITY

### BY HANNA JOHANSSON, TRANSLATED BY KIRA JOSEFSSON

Within the two hundred–odd pages of the novel *Antiquity*, written by Hanna Johansson and translated from the Swedish by Kira Josefsson, variants of the word *lonely* appear sixty-three times. Yet despite its pervasive loneliness, the book is heavily populated with characters. It follows an unnamed journalist as she travels to the Greek vacation home of an older, established, and self-obsessed artist, Helena, whom she once interviewed for a magazine. They are joined in Greece by Helena's brooding and buzz-cut teenage daughter, Olga. Tonally similar to Katie Kitamura's *Intimacies*, the novel features a narrator in a foreign land, steeped more in thought than in action. Mostly, Helena, Olga, and the unnamed narrator consume: hand-picked pomegranates, fresh squid, fragrant oranges, coffee. They take walks. They lie on the beach. Each page could be a still shot, capturing the precise mood of each "memory tableaux," as the narrator puts it, memorializing one exquisitely rendered moment after another.

*Antiquity* is crowded with loneliness. The narrator's loneliness is indiscriminate. It creeps up on her in the middle of watching a dance recital, while at dinner with others, in the midst of a commute. Readers quickly realize that this loneliness is of the narrator's own making. She constantly calculates the distance between herself and others, and she is paralyzed by her desire for an idealized closeness—with Helena, previous partners, and eventually Olga. In the narrator's hands, nearness is a function of both alienation and intimacy. She's around others, and observes them deeply, but still feels alone and unseen. While listening to the banalities of Helena's day, the narrator calls herself "an attentive rock."

About two-thirds of the way through the book, the narrator's desire for closeness shifts from Helena to Olga, and the two become romantically involved. The book's similarities to Vladimir Nabokov's *Lolita* are clear: an adult who

> **Publisher:** *Catapult* **Page count:** *224* **Price:** *$26.00* **Key quote:** *"I burned the ground she was walking on, I gave her an indelible memory, I erected a border, there would be no way back. I tore a hole in her history."* **Shelve next to:** *Julia May Jonas, Olivia Sudjic* **Unscientifically calculated reading time:** *Seven cherry Popsicles*

projects their fantasies of selfhood onto a child. The narrator uses the predatory language of Olga being "special." Predictably, the roles between lover and parent collapse. "I became her mother that night," the narrator recalls of one of her and Olga's clandestine encounters. "I rocked her. I nursed her." Like Dolores Haze, Olga is merely a thing, a beautiful statue with a "closed-eyed marble face." Thinking of Olga makes the narrator think of herself, a relationality that is actually a kind of individualism. "When I looked at her it was as if I saw myself," the narrator says. "When I kissed her I liberated her from something: her childhood, her mother."

Unlike the narrator, however, Olga is comfortable without anyone. "I don't want any friends," Olga says. In Olga's hands, aloneness becomes something to covet. Throughout the book, Johansson renders a genealogy of desire, placing intimacies side by side for the reader and the narrator to examine. A metaphor for this strategy comes from the sky: "I read: Orion is one of few constellations where many of the stars are actually near each other in space." Near but rarely touching: this is how the narrator lives her life, until a spark between her and Olga begins to grow.

As the summer wanes, the narrator increasingly concerns herself with the fantasy of her own impact. In other words, who will she be to Olga in the future? "She would keep living; I would have nothing to grieve," the narrator assesses. Again the narrator measures the weight that she and Olga will have on each other as if marking a doorway with each person's height. Ultimately, *Antiquity* maps out the crystallizing process of an impression, the places in a temporary affair where the fleshy stuff of love or lust hardens into narrative. "I was no longer in my own body," the narrator says as she is about to depart from Olga and Helena. "I was in the story I was telling myself. I was preparing a memory for later."

—*Rosa Boshier González*

117

*Illustration by Pete Gamlen*

# PRAIRIE, DRESSES, ART, OTHER

## BY DANIELLE DUTTON

When Danielle Dutton published *Margaret the First*, a historical novel about the seventeenth-century writer Duchess Margaret Cavendish, she reached back through time and pulled from the darkness a fellow writer who was vastly out of step with her own era, romantic and medieval in a new world of snide Renaissance men. Now, in Dutton's new book, *Prairie, Dresses, Art, Other*, a collection of fiction, essays, lists, notes, quotations, and a play, virtually every piece is in persistent conversation with other writers, mostly women, many dead. Dutton skips through inventive formal techniques as she integrates these other writers' styles, content, and sentences into her pieces. She even (I *love* this) includes herself as a writer to discuss. She quotes her own prior books and interviews, and explains them.

One fascinating piece is the tour-de-force "Sixty-Six Dresses I Have Read." The entire piece is made up of quotations from other writers writing about dresses! She strings together sixty-six descriptions of dresses that she apparently came across in an assortment of books, from Jean Rhys to Ovid to Sei Shōnagon to Joyelle McSweeney, defying anyone to call dress-writing frivolous (perhaps a little poke at David Shields's more self-serious *Reality Hunger*?). The effect is to bring forward as one reads the ongoing, centuries-long conversation about dresses, the abundant and intricate writing about them and all they signify, imply, hide, and reveal. A nod to tradition, a shadowy critique, the piece feels bold and audacious, yet quiet, understated, a show of respect, a salute from afar. Though not a single word is actually *by* Dutton, you feel her authorial hand hovering, choosing, arranging, taking sides, luxuriating, laughing, having something to say. It is a beautiful piece, daring and intimate, as the best dresses are.

Another way this collection feels like a leap forward is in Dutton's passionate integration of our present world and all its troubles. Dutton has lived in the Midwest for twenty years, on prairieland that is "one of the least conserved habitats on

**Publisher:** *Coffee House Press* **Page count:** *176* **Price:** *$17.95* **Key quote:** *"They are driving upside down on the bottom of the planet."* **Shelve next to:** *Hiroko Oyamada, Virginia Woolf, Emily Carroll* **Unscientifically calculated reading time:** *One long flight delay and a hot bath when you finally arrive*

the planet." There are tiny bits of it left here and there, "prairie remnants." She takes great pains to note these scraps, the flora and fauna that survive. "The songs of various birds are bouncing off the river, springing through her hair: *Louisiana waterthrush, yellow-breasted chat.*" But the crazy landscape of our contemporary world keeps butting onto the page. "It's the hottest week in the world," a narrator announces. Jarring images of oil refineries, snippets of horrific non sequitur news stories, constant references to video games, leaf blowers, websites, MAGA hats, man-made mega-dams, phones, fires, heat, drought: she creates a collage—disaster scenario alongside peaceful prairie remnant. She creates on the page the disorienting and surreal feeling of being alive today, with our crushing end-of-the-world barkers in our pockets.

How the world has changed since the Brontë sisters wrote of long walks over the moors, or Virginia Woolf of flowers, trees, water, sky. The texture of those writers is all over these pages, and you can almost hear Dutton talking to them, saying, *Look what's happened!* Saying, *Is there a future?*

Dutton's greatest powers are her immense skill with language; her exacting attention to image, sound, phrase; her commitment to creating strangeness and newness. Every sentence rewrites a million lesser sentences before it. On one page, she writes the history of the universe in a sentence: "Once upon a time all matter and light were one—then the stars and then the fireflies and then the grass." A few pages later, she breaks into a boundless, wild list-song, celebrating light: "There are so many different kinds: forest light; harbor light; light between trees in a grove; cloud light; Martian light, alarm clock light; pink; the light at a European football game, or on a piece of bread; rainbow light; bomb light, laundered sheets; the sun; blinding light of a *daffodil*…" Light was the first thing to be here; it will be the last to go. It is still safe to love it and all it illuminates: the world. Her list keeps going.

—*Deb Olin Unferth*

*Illustration by Pete Gamlen*

# COVER TO COVER

SURVEYING THE COVERS OF GREAT BOOKS AS THEY CHANGE ACROSS TIME AND COUNTRY.
IN THIS ISSUE: *THE LOTTERY* BY SHIRLEY JACKSON

*Compiled by Claire Fairtlough*

**UNITED STATES**
*Picador*
*2019*

**UNITED STATES**
*Lion*
*1950*

**UNITED STATES**
*Avon*
*1960*

**UNITED KINGDOM**
*Penguin*
*2022*

**UNITED STATES**
*Avon*
*1969*

**SPAIN**
*Debolsillo*
*2015*

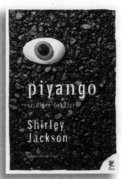

**TURKEY**
*Siren Yayınları*
*2020*

**UNITED KINGDOM**
*Penguin*
*2009*

**UNITED STATES**
*FSG*
*2005*

**UNITED STATES**
*Wildside Press*
*2018*

**SPAIN**
*Alfaguara*
*2022*

**RUSSIA**
*Eksmo*
*2013*

**CHINA**
*Yilin Press*
*2019*

**GERMANY**
*Diogenes*
*1989*

**UNITED STATES**
*Avon*
*1965*

# THE PUZZLE OF INCREDIBLY WIDE AND DEEP KNOWLEDGE

### IF YOU COMPLETE THIS PUZZLE, YOU ARE A GENERALIST OF BROAD SKILL AND GREAT RENOWN

*by Ada Nicolle; edited by Benjamin Tausig*

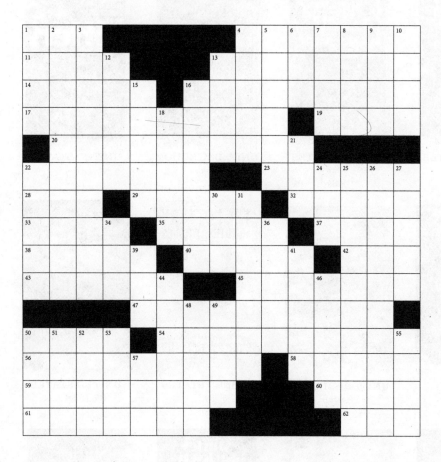

37. With 40-Across, highly venomous mollusc
38. A male one is called a boar
40. See 37-Across
42. Bit of mockery
43. Color container
45. Some of its genre categories include "dub-steppe" and "J-alt"
47. Queen's adviser?
50. Some Logic Pro plug-ins
54. Somewhat, cutely
56. Have an arm for each hand
58. Drug lord Carrillo Fuentes known as "El Señor de los Cielos"
59. Once
60. Food brand that once collaborated with Lego
61. Top, ungrammatically and redundantly
62. {"This", "in", "Python"}

## DOWN

1. Depiction on a lab poster
2. Record holder for the longest-running mini-game series
3. "Same"
4. Dog
5. Portmanteau describing a door-opening sound
6. MSNBC correspondent Melber
7. Spartan queen of Greek myth
8. Dog
9. They may be affected by congestion
10. House work, briefly
12. Fourth word of K'naan's "Wavin' Flag"
13. Prize holder at an arcade
15. Impact sound
16. Overcharges
18. Alpine flower
21. It's relative?
22. "Don't tell me this is happening..."
24. One with a dialogue tree, in video games: Abbr.
25. Company acquisitions?
26. Cooler for a student, maybe
27. Words for the late
30. Dynasty that followed Qin
31. Moved involuntarily
34. Game changer, at times?
36. Nurse
39. Compliment with a shaka sign, maybe
41. Contraction that anagrams to a choir section
44. VIA vehicles
46. Plant made up of two pronouns
48. Patronized, in a sense
49. Has great chemistry (with)
50. Not much, as of cream
51. Mona Lisa was one
52. Word before "port" or "phrase"
53. Opening
55. Mastodon post, formerly
57. "___ betide ..." ("A pox on ...")

## ACROSS

1. "Frère," peut-être
4. Collection of hymns
11. Common "antojito" ("little craving")
13. Put together, together
14. Exams that might simulate real-word application
16. Grand ___ (Disney World resort)
17. Memorization technique in which memories are associated with rooms
19. "And ANOTHER thing I'm mad about ..."
20. Uncowed response
22. Modify an organ, perhaps
23. Triumphant board game command
28. ___ Leonard (sheet music publisher)
29. Basketball fouls that may be assessed to coaches, briefly
32. Render unwatchable
33. ___ school
35. Takes out of the field

*(answers on page 128)*

# COPYEDITING THE CLASSICS

*by Caitlin Van Dusen*

*THE SUN ALSO RISES* (1925)
*by* ERNEST HEMINGWAY

I had coffee and the papers in bed and then dressed and took my bathing-suit down to the beach. Everything was fresh and cool and damp in the early morning…. Some boot-blacks sat together under a tree talking to a soldier. The soldier only had one arm. The tide was in and there was a good breeze and a surf on the beach.

I undressed in one of the bath-cabins, crossed the narrow line of beach and went into the water. I swam out, trying to swim through the rollers, but having to dive sometimes. Then in the quiet water I turned and floated. Floating, the sky was the only thing I saw, and I felt the drop and lift of the swells. I swam back to the surf and coasted in, face down, on a big roller, then turned and swum, trying to keep in the trough and have a wave not break over me. It made me tired, swimming in the trough, and I turned and swam out to the raft. The water was buoyant and cold. It felt as though you could never sink. I swam slowly, it seemed like a long swim with the low tide, and then pulled upon the raft and sat, dripping, on the boards which were becoming hot in the sun…. Off on the right, almost closing the harbor was a green hill with a castle….

I sat in the sun and watched the bathers on the beach. They looked very small. After a while I stood up, gripped with my toes on the edge of the raft as it tipped with my weight, and dove cleanly and deeply, to come up through the lightning water, blew the salt water out of my head, and swam slowly and steadily into shore.

(answers on page 128)

*Follow The Chicago Manual of Style, 17th edition. Please ignore unusual spellings, hyphenations, and capitalizations, and the that/which distinction. All are characteristic of the author's style and time.*

# JACKET CAPTCHA
CAN YOU IDENTIFY THESE NINE BOOK COVERS?

# COMPLETE ME

HOW WELL DO YOU KNOW JENNY SLATE? FILL IN THIS PARAGRAPH OF
BIOGRAPHICAL TRIVIA, PENNED BY THE AUTHOR HERSELF.

I was born in _____, Massachusetts, in 198_. Before I was a writer, actor, and

comedian, I was the _____ of my high school. I went to _____

University, where I studied _____ and comp. lit. There are other writers in

my family! My _____ is a writer, too, but he writes mostly poetry. We co-

wrote a book, _____ ___ _____, which is a collection of stories, essays, and

poems about the house I grew up in. When my book *Little Weirds* was published

by _____, _____ ___ _____ in 201_, I did an interview with my editor,

____ _____, about what the process of writing the book was like for me.

I actually finished the book after a _____-day editing session at my editor's house

during her maternity leave! We edited large parts of the book by reading it out

loud. We landed on the title because we thought, They're not _____; they're

not _____; they're Little Weirds.

# INTERNATIONAL BESTSELLER LISTS

*See what the rest of the world is reading in this regular feature, which highlights a rotating cast of countries in each issue.*

COMPILED BY ELLIOTE MUIR, ACCORDING TO 2023 ANNUAL LISTS

## NEW ZEALAND

1. **Birnam Wood by Eleanor Catton.** *A guerilla gardening collective and an American billionaire vie for abandoned farmland in rural New Zealand.*

2. **The Axeman's Carnival by Catherine Chidgey.** *Human and animal worlds collide when the wife of a struggling farmer takes in an injured magpie.*

3. **Sisters Under the Rising Sun by Heather Morris.** *During World War II, an English musician and a Welsh Australian nurse join forces to survive as prisoners of war.*

4. **Kāwai: For Such a Time as This by Monty Soutar.** *This historical novel is the first in a trilogy about one Māori man adventuring through precolonial Aotearoa.*

5. **P.S. Come to Italy by Nicky Pellegrino.** *Two grieving strangers find solace in a romance that spans from New Zealand to Italy.*

6. **Pet by Catherine Chidgey.** *Students who compete for their teacher's favor and attention face dark, thirty-year-long ramifications.*

7. **Everything Is Beautiful and Everything Hurts by Josie Shapiro.** *An outcast at school, Mickey discovers a passion for long-distance running, only to find it comes with its own painful challenges.*

8. **The Bone Tree by Airana Ngarewa.** *Orphaned siblings confront an unjust society and its impact on their family history as they fight to remain together.*

9. **Lioness by Emily Perkins.** *As her world of privilege begins to crumble, Therese gains a new perspective on life when she becomes friends with her free-spirited neighbor.*

10. **The Girl from London by Olivia Spooner.** *Sixty years after a schoolteacher helped children evacuate World War II England, a young woman en route to London rediscovers her story.*

## MEXICO

1. **El viento conoce mi nombre (The Wind Knows My Name) by Isabel Allende.** *Switching between historical periods decades apart, this novel tells the story of two children who are forced to separate from their families and make new connections amid political conflict.*

2. **El viaje de los colibríes (The Journey of the Hummingbirds) by Sue Zurita.** *Seeking a fresh start in a new city, a young woman ends up on a years-long journey of self-discovery.*

3. **Todo lo que nunca fuimos (All That We Never Were) by Alice Kellen.** *Following a tragic car accident, a grieving daughter falls for her brother's best friend.*

4. **Cuando no queden más estrellas para contar (When There Are No Stars Left to Count) by María Martínez.** *When a critical accident derails a ballerina's career, she must construct a new identity without the guidance of her grandmother.*

5. **Pedro páramo (Pedro Páramo) by Juan Rulfo.** *In this seminal Latin American novel, a young man in search of his father comes across a ghost town full of spectral inhabitants.*

6. **Las batallas en el desierto (Battles in the Desert) by José Emilio Pacheco.** *After World War II in a rapidly changing Mexico City, a teenager falls catastrophically in love for the first time.*

7. **Un cuento perfecto (A Perfect Short Story) by Elísabet Benavent.** *A romance forms between a couch-surfing bartender and a bride who has just run away from her high-society wedding.*

8. **La cabeza de mi padre (My Father's Head) by Alma Delia Murillo.** *Many years after her father abandoned the family, a forty-year-old woman searches Mexico to find him.*

9. **Cien años de soledad (One Hundred Years of Solitude) by Gabriel García Márquez.** *This renowned work of magic realism tracks many generations of the Buendía family.*

10. **Extrañas (Strangers) by Guillermo Arriaga.** *Following the Scientific Revolution, a British nobleman sets out to meet the world's leading thinkers.*

## ITALY

1. **La portalettere (The Postman) by Francesca Giannone.** *Ostracized by her new neighbors in southern Italy, a northern woman becomes the town's postman.*

2. **Tre ciotole: Rituali per un anno di crisi (Three Bowls: Rituals for a Year of Crisis) by Michela Murgia.** *The lives of this book's twelve protagonists are linked as each undergoes major changes in the midst of the COVID-19 pandemic.*

3. **La vita intima (Intimate Life) by Niccolò Ammaniti.** *The wife of Italy's prime minister enjoys a seemingly perfect life until a video from the past puts her position in jeopardy.*

4. **Come d'aria (Like Air) by Ada D'Adamo.** *In this memoir, a mother fights a tumor while trying to care for her disabled daughter.*

5. **Tutto è qui per te (Everything Is Here for You) by Fabio Volo.** *After dating in their twenties, a couple goes their separate ways and reunites years later.*

6. **ELP (PLA) by Antonio Manzini.** *Two investigations with ties to environmental protests unfold simultaneously in the nineteenth installment of this Italian crime series.*

7. **L'educazione delle farfalle (The Education of Butterflies) by Donato Carrisi.** *Career-minded Serena reckons with the challenges of motherhood as she searches for her missing daughter.*

8. **Le otto montagne (Eight Mountains) by Paolo Cognetti.** *A Milanese boy befriends one of the locals in the mountain town where his parents fell in love.*

9. **Due cuori in affitto (Two Hearts for Rent) by Felicia Kingsley.** *Two strangers with nothing in common find themselves sharing a summer home in the Hamptons, in New York.*

10. **Fabbricante di lacrime (The Tearsmith) by Erin Doom.** *The author of this novel about an inhumane orphanage first gained recognition on the writing platform Wattpad.*

## IRELAND

1. **Strange Sally Diamond by Liz Nugent.** *When her father dies, a traumatized and reclusive woman throws him out with the trash.*

2. **Prophet Song by Paul Lynch.** *The winner of the 2023 Booker Prize, this novel follows a scientist in dystopic Ireland as she scrambles to protect her family after her husband's arrest.*

3. **The Bee Sting by Paul Murray.** *Once prosperous and cheerfully normal, the Barnes family flounders in small-town Ireland in the wake of an economic downturn.*

4. **Aisling Ever After by Emer McLysaght and Sarah Breen.** *In the fifth and final book in this cowritten series, Aisling weighs the American dream against her Irish roots.*

5. **My Father's House by Joseph O'Connor.** *A man helps Jews and Allied prisoners escape occupied Italy during World War II in this book based on a true story.*

6. **Small Things Like These by Claire Keegan.** *In the weeks before Christmas, a hardworking coal merchant reckons with the power of the church in small-town Ireland.*

7. **No One Saw a Thing by Andrea Mara.** *After being separated from her young daughters on the London tube and finding only one of them, Sive embarks on a frantic search for the still-missing six-year-old.*

8. **So Late in the Day: Stories of Women and Men by Claire Keegan.** *These three short stories explore the darkness that lurks in relationships between men and women.*

9. **Body of Truth by Marie Cassidy.** *A new-to-town detective investigates the murder of a prominent true-crime podcaster.*

10. **Old God's Time by Sebastian Barry.** *The solitary retirement of detective Tom Kettle is disturbed by an unsolved case from his past.*

## PUBLICATIONS

**HIGHLY RECOMMENDED—** *Believer* contributor Lauren Markham's new book, *A Map of Future Ruins*, is now available. In a starred review, *Kirkus* says, "A remarkable, unnerving, and cautionary portrait of a global immigration crisis."

**EAT THE RICH—**In a future where rain is reserved for the ultra-rich, the world's only umbrella maker is framed for a high-profile murder. C.R. Foster's debut novel, *The Rain Artist*, is *Succession* meets *The Fifth Element*, with a glorious and gory twist. Find your copy wherever queer lit is sold or see moonstruck-books .com for more.

Read **COOLEST AMERICAN STORIES** editor Mark Wish's 4th novel, the literary noir mystery NECESSARY DEEDS! Called "irresistible and addictive" by NYT bestseller Tim Johnton, "a high-stakes noir and a taut tale of jealousy" by international bestseller Laura McHugh, "a novel to be devoured, then savored" by Daniel Torday, "sly, sharp, and satirical" by Alan Orloff, and "nuanced and wryly observed" and "unputdownable" by Tish Cohen. Leland Cheuk called it "necessary reading," and PEN Award winner Morgan Talty of NIGHT OF THE LIVING REZ fame summed up his praise of it by saying, "Any reader would love this." https://amzn .to/3SM2K6a

**SEARCHING FOR SASQUATCH—**In his debut book, *The Secret History of Bigfoot: Field Notes on a North American Monster*, frequent *Believer* contributor and self-diagnosed skeptic John O'Connor adventures into the zany and secretive world of "cryptozoology." A starred review from *Publishers Weekly* called it "a winning portrait of America at its weirdest."

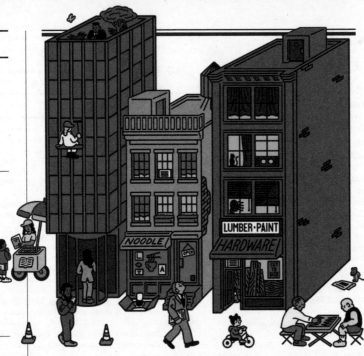

# CLASSIFIEDS

*Believer Classifieds cost $2 per word. They can be placed by emailing classifieds@thebeliever.net. All submissions subject to editorial approval. No results guaranteed.*

## BELIEVER-RELATED

Back issues of *The Believer* available, including some rare issues (2007–2015)—Destinationbooks .net  https://bit.ly/4aJaWL7

## FELICITATIONS

**SPEEDY RECOVERY** from your surgery, Big Mike. Proud you took charge and tackled that hernia. I got a few cold beers and a DiGiorno's waiting for you at my place whenever you're up for a visit. Always here for you brother.

**THE BIG 25!** The happiest of anniversaries to our favorite scrapbooking, jazz-playing, paella-making, crossword-ing, marathon-running, aqua jogging dads. Shaun & Tim, we love you!

**OLIVIA, QUEEN OF PUNS—** On your 32nd birthday, may your jokes be sharper and your puns punnier. Here's to another year of groans and eye rolls from all of us who adore your weird sense of humor. Happy Birthday, Olivia!

**ENGAGED!** Our biggest congratulations to Astrid & Jacob—from college classmates to adventurous, entrepreneurial couple, we are so excited to celebrate you both and watch your lives together unfold. Much love from Aunt TJ & Uncle Jim

**HAPPY 20TH TO OUR COSMIC EXPLORER:** To Sarah, who's more fascinating than the farthest star and dearer than the rarest comet. May your day be filled with love and stardust. From your Earth-bound family.

**CONGRATULATIONS**, Daniel, for following through with your decision to go to vet school. You've got a big heart, brother, and I know you're gonna make a lot of animals and pet owners very happy. —Ted

## SUBMISSIONS

**2025 PRESS 53 AWARD FOR POETRY—**$1,000, publication, and 53 copies awarded to an outstanding, unpublished collection of poems. Open to poets 18 and older who live in the US. Press 53 Poetry Series Editor Tom Lombardo will judge. All prizes awarded upon publication. Open April 1 to July 31. Winner and finalists announced no later than November 1. Reading fee: $30. Complete information at www .press53.com/award-for-poetry

**PARTY LIKE WE'RE IN OUR 30s—**In July of our 30th year, Sarabande will be home by 8pm, blanketed in cats, reading your manuscript submissions of poetry, short fiction, and essays, as well as translation proposals. For more info and to submit, visit sarabandebooks.org.

## SERVICES

**PENCILHOUSE—**We read WIPs and write feedback on 'em, simple as that. FREE submissions monthly, capacity-capped; $6/mo for submit-whenever, cap-free subs. ALWAYS SEEKING VOLUNTEER CRITICS. pencilhouse.org (http: //pencilhouse.org/)

**WRITE UNBORING PLAYS—** Classes, accountability, and consults for inquisitive, rebellious dramatists. Shake it up. katetarker.com

## MISSED CONNECTIONS

**MEG—**just finished *The Bee Sting*. Nobody writes quite like the Irish. Many thanks for the recommendation (I would be happy to take more should you have them—that was quite a pile you had on your table at the coffee shop). Write back, if you wish, through this Classifieds page. Yours, Alice

*Illustrations by Tomi Um*

# NOTES ON OUR CONTRIBUTORS

**Ann Beattie** is a member of the American Academy of Arts and Letters. In 2023, Godine published her essays, *More to Say: Essays and Appreciations*, and Scribner published her new story collection, *Onlookers*. She lives with her husband, Lincoln Perry, in Maine and Virginia.

**Eula Biss** is the author of four books, most recently *Having and Being Had*. Her work has been translated into a dozen languages and has been recognized by a National Book Critics Circle Award, a Guggenheim Fellowship, and a 21st Century Award from the Chicago Public Library.

**Rosa Boshier González** is a writer and editor whose fiction, essays, and art criticism appear in *Guernica*, *Catapult*, *Literary Hub*, *The New York Times*, *Artforum*, *The Guardian*, *The Washington Post*, and the *Los Angeles Review of Books*, among other publications. She serves as the editor in chief of *Gulf Coast Journal*.

**Alan Chazaro** is the author of *This Is Not a Frank Ocean Cover Album*, *Piñata Theory*, and *Notes from the Eastern Span of the Bay Bridge*. He is a graduate of June Jordan's Poetry for the People program at the University of California at Berkeley, and a former Lawrence Ferlinghetti Poetry Fellow at the University of San Francisco. He was proudly raised by Mexican immigrants in the Bay Area and is currently a staff writer for KQED Arts and Culture.

**Benjamin Cohen** lives and works in Easton, Pennsylvania. He is a former film critic for *The Granville Sentinel* and a current professor at Lafayette College.

**Yvonne Conza** is a writer in Miami. She has words in *Longreads*, *Michigan Quarterly Review*, *Catapult*, *Joyland*, *Pleiades*, *Blue Mesa Review*, and other outlets. She is the assistant nonfiction editor for *Pithead Chapel* and coauthor of the user-friendly dog-training guide *Training for Both Ends of the Leash*. Find her on Instagram at @yvonneconza.

**Emma Copley Eisenberg** is a writer of fiction and nonfiction. Her debut novel, *Housemates*, will be published by Hogarth Press in May 2024, and she is also the author of *The Third Rainbow Girl*, which was named a *New York Times* Notable Book and Editors' Choice of 2020 and was nominated for an Edgar Award, a Lambda Literary Award, and an Anthony Award. Her work has appeared in *The New York Times*, *McSweeney's Quarterly*, *Granta*, *Esquire*, and many other publications. She lives in Philadelphia, where she cofounded Blue Stoop, a community hub for the literary arts.

**Natalie Eilbert** is the author of *Overland*, *Indictus*, and *Swan Feast*. A recipient of a grant in poetry from the National Endowment for the Arts, and a former Jay C. and Ruth Halls Poetry Fellow at the Wisconsin Institute of Creative Writing, she lives and works as a journalist in Green Bay, Wisconsin.

**Daniel Elkind** is author of *Chizhevsky's Chandelier*. He lives in Atlanta.

**Veronique Greenwood** is a journalist and essayist who lives in England. Her work has appeared in publications including *The New York Times*, *The Atlantic*, and *The Boston Globe*.

**George Gene Gustines** has worked at *The New York Times* since 1990 and began writing about comic books in 2002. It was lonely at the beginning but is now much more competitive, thanks to the influence of comics on animated series, live-action television shows, films, and more. His career goals are landing a solo story on the front page and reaching a thousand bylines.

**Daniel Halpern** is the author of nine collections of poetry, most recently *Something Shining*. For twenty-five years, he edited the international literary magazine *Antaeus*, which he cofounded in Tangier with Paul Bowles. He has received fellowships from the Guggenheim Foundation and the National Endowment for the Arts, as well as the first Editor's Award, given by *Poets & Writers*, and the 2015 Maxwell E. Perkins Award. From 1975 to 1995 he taught in the graduate writing program at Columbia University, which he chaired for many years. And in 1978, with James Michener, he founded the National Poetry Series, which oversees the publication of five books of poetry each year. Halpern was founder, president, and publisher of Ecco, and is now an executive editor at Alfred A. Knopf.

**Nick Hilden** writes about the arts, politics, science, and travel for the likes of *The Washington Post*, *Esquire*, *Publishers Weekly*, *Scientific American*, *The Millions*, *Afar*, *National Geographic*, and many other publications.

**Lexi Kent-Monning** is an alumna of the Tyrant Books workshop Mors Tua Vita Mea in Sezze Romano, Italy, taught by Giancarlo DiTrapano and Chelsea Hodson. Her writing has been published in *X-R-A-Y*, *Joyland*, *Black Lipstick*, *Little Engines*, and elsewhere. Lexi's debut novel, *The Burden of Joy*, is available through Rejection Letters press.

**Rachel Khong** is the author of the novels *Goodbye, Vitamin* and *Real Americans*, forthcoming from Knopf in April 2024. She was born in Malaysia and lives in Los Angeles.

**Jordan Kisner** is the author of the essay collection *Thin Places*, and the creator of the podcast *Thresholds*. She is also a contributing writer for *The New York Times Magazine* and *The Atlantic*. She lives in New York.

**Zefyr Lisowski** is the author of two poetry collections, *Blood Box* and *Girl Work*. Her essay collection about horror movies, exes, and love is forthcoming from Harper Perennial in fall 2025. She is a 2023 recipient of a New York State Council on the Arts / New York Foundation for the Arts Fellowship in nonfiction.

**Kristen Martin** is a cultural critic based in Philadelphia. Her debut narrative nonfiction book, *The Sun Won't Come Out Tomorrow*, will be published by Bold Type Books in 2025. She has written for *The New York Times Magazine*, *The Washington Post*, NPR, *The Atlantic*, *The New Republic*, and other publications.

**Christian Meesey** is an illustrator and caricaturist whose clients include Disney, Warner Bros., IDW, Cosmic Lion, and Image Comics. His book *Time Shopper* (written by Tony Fleecs) was a 2023 National Cartoonists Society Reuben Award nominee for Best Graphic Novel. He lives and draws somewhere in the Midwest.

**Michael Prior** is a writer, teacher, and editor. His most recent book of poems, *Burning Province*, won the Canada-Japan Literary Award and the BC and Yukon Book Prizes' Dorothy Livesay Poetry Prize. He is also the author of *Model Disciple*, which was named one of the best books of the year by the Canadian Broadcasting Corporation.

**Meara Sharma** is a writer and artist whose work has appeared in *Guernica*, *Frieze*, *Ambit*, *VICE*, *The New York Times*, *The Washington Post*, and elsewhere. She was the founding editor in chief of *Adi*, a literary magazine of global politics. With roots in Massachusetts and India, she currently lives in Scotland.

**Susan Steinberg**'s most recent books of fiction are *Machine* and *Spectacle*, both from Graywolf Press. She lives in San Francisco.

**Alessandro Tersigni** is a critic and essayist who writes about art, culture, nature, and buildings. He's excited equally by eclecticism and tradition, form and content, suburbs and Georgian manors.

**Madeleine Thien** is the author of four books, most recently, *Do Not Say We Have Nothing*, shortlisted for the 2016 Booker Prize. She lives in Montreal.

**Deb Olin Unferth** is the author of six books, including the novel *Barn 8*. She has received a Guggenheim Fellowship and four Pushcart Prizes, and was a finalist for the National Book Critics Circle Award. A professor at the University of Texas at Austin, she also directs the Pen City Writers, a small creative writing program at a south Texas penitentiary.

**Tony Wolf** is a comics creator and actor based in the New York City area. He has created several comics journalism pieces for *The New York Times*. He has also appeared on *The Marvelous Mrs. Maisel*, *Comedy Central*, and *The Blacklist*. Cosmic Lion recently published his short-story collection *Tales from the Wolf*.

**Bryce Woodcock** is a critical writer, musician, and audio engineer currently pursuing an MA in aesthetics and politics at CalArts. His research focuses on conspiracy theory and network culture. He has previously served as an editorial assistant for Rejection Letters Press.

# IN THE NEXT ISSUE

*Not all contents are guaranteed; replacements will be satisfying*

## SOLUTIONS TO THIS ISSUE'S GAMES AND PUZZLES

### CROSSWORD
(Page 120)

### JACKET CAPTCHA
(Page 122)

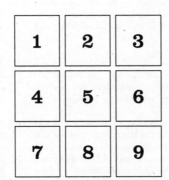

1. *Hangman* by Maya Binyam
2. *The Rings of Saturn* by W. G. Sebald
3. *Speedboat* by Renata Adler
4. *Fascination* by Kevin Killian
5. *Ways of Seeing* by John Berger
6. *Counternarratives* by John Keene
7. *Postcards from the Edge* by Carrie Fisher
8. *Scented Gardens for the Blind* by Janet Frame
9. *Orientalism* by Edward W. Said

### COMPLETE ME
(Page 123)

1. Boston
2. 2
3. valedictorian
4. Columbia
5. English
6. father
7. *About the House*
8. Little, Brown and Company
9. 9
10. Jean Garrett
11. four
12. essays
13. stories

---

### COPYEDITING THE CLASSICS (Page 121)

I had coffee and the papers in bed and then dressed and took my bathing-suit down to the beach. Everything was fresh and cool and damp in the early morning.... Some bootblacks sat together under a tree talking to a soldier. The soldier only had (1) one arm. The tide was in and there was a good breeze and a surf on the beach.

I undressed in one of the bath-cabins, crossed the narrow line of beach and went into the water. I swam out, trying to swim through the rollers, but having to dive sometimes. Then in the quiet water I turned and floated. Floating, the sky was the only thing I saw, and I felt (2) the drop and lift of the swells. I swam back to the surf and coasted in, face down, on a big roller, then turned and swum (3), trying to keep in the trough and have a wave not (4) break over me. It made me tired, swimming in the trough, and I turned and swam out to the raft. The water was buoyant and cold. It felt as though you could never sink. I swam slowly, it seemed like a long swim with the low tide (5), and then pulled upon (6) the raft and sat, dripping, on the boards which (7) were becoming hot in the sun.... Off on the right, almost closing the harbor (8) was a green hill with a castle....

I sat in the sun and watched the bathers on the beach. They looked very small. After a while I stood up, gripped with my toes on the edge of the raft as it tipped with my weight, and dove cleanly and deeply, to come up through the lightning (9) water, blew the salt water out of my head, and swam slowly and steadily into (10) shore.

1. had only. *Only* should directly precede the word it modifies—in this case, *arm* rather than *had*.
2. Floating, I saw only the sky, and felt. This is a dangling participle: the narrator ("I") was floating, not the sky.
3. swam. The past participle of *to swim* is *swum*. The simple past is *swam*.
4. not have a wave. *Not* should modify the entire verb phrase.
5. high tide. This is a plot continuity error. Just above he says "the tide was in," meaning high tide, and not enough time has passed for the tide to be low.
6. up on. It can be easy to overlook closed-up words that should have spaces, especially when the closed-up word is also a word.
7. that. *That* is restrictive: it indicates that certain boards are becoming hot while others are not, which is what is meant here. *Which* is nonrestrictive, meaning it's introducing information that is not essential to the meaning.
8. , [comma] A comma is needed here to enclose "almost closing the harbor," which is an aside.
9. lightening. *Lightning* goes with thunder; *lightening* means "becoming lighter."
10. in to. *Into* is a preposition that indicates movement; the *in* in *in to* is used adverbially to modify *swim*.